AMERICAN ★ HISTORY

The TRANSCONTINENTAL RAILROAD

Connecting the Nation

By Therese Harasymiw

Portions of this book originally appeared in
The Transcontinental Railroad by Michael V. Uschan.

LUCENT PRESS

Published in 2018 by
Lucent Press, an Imprint of Greenhaven Publishing, LLC
353 3rd Avenue
Suite 255
New York, NY 10010

Designer: Deanna Paternostro
Editor: Siyavush Saidian

Library of Congress Cataloging-in-Publication Data

Names: Harasymiw, Therese.
Title: The Transcontinental Railroad: connecting the nation / Therese Harasymiw.
Description: New York : Lucent Press, 2018. | Series: American history | Includes index.
Identifiers: ISBN 9781534561373 (library bound) | ISBN 9781534561380 (ebook)
Subjects: LCSH: Pacific railroads–History–Juvenile literature. | Railroads–West (U.S.)–History–Juvenile literature. | Railroads–United States–History–Juvenile literature. | Railroads–United States–Design and construction–History–Juvenile literature. | United States–Territorial expansion–Juvenile literature.
Classification: LCC TF25.P23 H315 2018 | DDC 385.0978'09034–dc23

Printed in the United States of America

CPSIA compliance information: Batch #BS17KL: For further information contact Greenhaven Publishing LLC, New York, New York at 1-844-317-7404.

Please visit our website, www.greenhavenpublishing.com. For a free color catalog of all our high-quality books, call toll free 1-844-317-7404 or fax 1-844-317-7405.

Contents

Foreword

The United States is a relatively young country. It has existed as its own nation for more than 200 years, but compared to nations such as China that have existed since ancient times, it is still in its infancy. However, the United States has grown and accomplished much since its birth in 1776. What started as a loose confederation of former British colonies has grown into a major world power whose influence is felt around the globe.

How did the United States manage to develop into a global superpower in such a short time? The answer lies in a close study of its unique history. The story of America is unlike any other—filled with colorful characters, a variety of exciting settings, and events too incredible to be anything other than true.

Too often, the experience of history is lost among the basic facts: names, dates, places, laws, treaties, and battles. These fill countless textbooks, but they are rarely compelling on their own. Far more interesting are the stories that surround those

basic facts. It is in discovering those stories that students are able to see history as a subject filled with life—and a subject that says as much about the present as it does about the past.

The titles in this series allow readers to immerse themselves in the action at pivotal historical moments. They also encourage readers to discuss complex issues in American history—many of which still affect Americans today. These include racism, states' rights, civil liberties, and many other topics that are in the news today but have their roots in the earliest days of America. As such, readers are encouraged to think critically about history and current events.

Each title is filled with excellent tools for research and analysis. Fully cited quotations from historical figures, letters, speeches, and documents provide students with firsthand accounts of major events. Primary sources bring authority to the text, as well. Sidebars highlight these quotes and primary sources, as well as interesting figures and events. Annotated bibliographies allow students to locate and evaluate sources for further information on the subject.

A deep understanding of America's past is necessary to understand its present and its future. Sometimes you have to look back to see how to best move forward, and that's certainly true when writing the next chapter in the American story.

Setting the Scene:

1803
The United States acquires the Louisiana Territory from France.

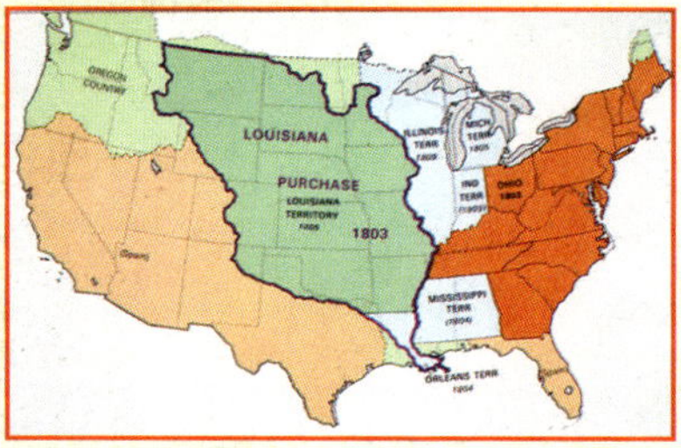

1846–1850
Great Britain and the United States sign the Oregon Treaty; the Treaty of Guadalupe Hidalgo ends the Mexican-American War; California becomes the 31st state.

1803 | 1845 | 1846–1850 | 1853

1845
Texas is annexed into the United States, becoming the 28th state.

1853
Congress authorizes the U.S. Army Corps of Topographical Engineers to map a route from the Mississippi River to the Pacific Ocean for a transcontinental railroad.

A Timeline

1859
The territory of Oregon becomes the 33rd state.

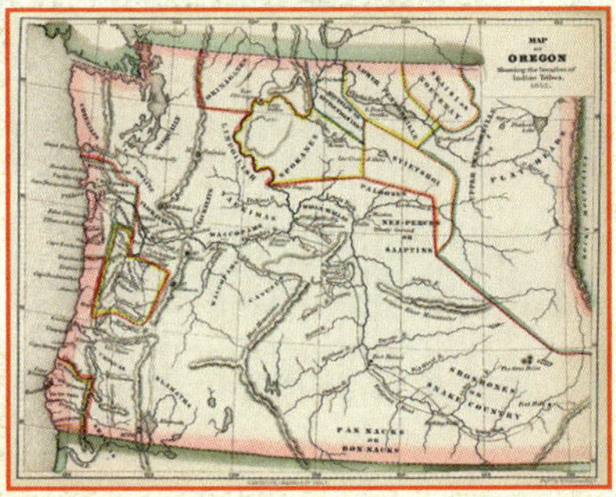

1869
The transcontinental railroad is completed.

1859 | 1861–1865 | 1869

1861–1865
The American Civil War begins; President Abraham Lincoln signs the Pacific Railway Act to provide government funding to build a transcontinental railroad; the American Civil War ends.

Introduction

A RAILWAY FROM COAST TO COAST

The date was May 10, 1869. An area of plains near Salt Lake City, Utah, named Promontory Summit was the location of the historic occasion. Two railroad crews had met at the locale and were about to join nearly 1,800 miles (2,897 km) of track they had laid across the United States, connecting the western and eastern halves of the nation for the first time. This railway—the transcontinental railroad—was almost finished. Officials drove a golden spike into the final tie.

Six years prior, the railroads had begun laying track with equally celebratory fanfare. The Central Pacific Railroad's work officially began in January 1863, in Sacramento, California. Governor Leland Stanford was one of several speakers to mark the occasion. He predicted the venture would "strengthen the ties of nationality, and advance with giant strides the prosperity of the State and of our country."[1] This statement was especially meaningful in the midst of the American Civil War, which was still raging at the time. To the East, the Union Pacific Railroad held a groundbreaking ceremony nearly a year later, in December 1863, near Omaha, Nebraska. Investor George Francis Train called the transcontinental venture the "greatest enterprise under God."[2]

Both these observances were merely ceremonial, as the two railroads were not yet equipped or staffed enough to begin their work just yet. This was no ordinary track to lay, and its obstacles were many. Modern-day engineers assert that the transcontinental railroad was the most complex construction project that any country in the world had attempted in the 19th century. It required detailed planning and massive amounts of money, equipment, and manpower. Though it would take

This photograph was captured at the celebration of the completion of the transcontinental railroad in Promontory Summit, Utah.

years, the completed railroad—when connected to the existing eastern railroads—yielded the enormous impact on the nation that many had forecast and anticipated. It also forever altered the physical and cultural terrain across the central and western United States.

Crossing the Continent

The transcontinental railroad was a joint effort of two separate railroad companies. The Union Pacific built 1,086 miles (1,748 km) of track heading west from Omaha. The Central Pacific laid 690 miles (1,110 km) of rails heading east from Sacramento. After years of hard, exhausting, and sometimes dangerous labor, workers for the two railroads connected the two lines in Promontory Summit, Utah. For the first time, the nation had a continuous railroad system stretching all the way across the North American continent.

The monumental task of building this historic railroad required a workforce of some 25,000 laborers, many of whom died while accomplishing this difficult task. These workers built a total of 1,776 miles (2,858 km) of track across stretches of hot and arid desert, swift-running rivers, deep ravines, and towering mountains. They constructed wooden bridges hundreds of feet high to cross huge canyons, chiseled out paths for the railroad down the sides of steep mountains, and, when necessary, blasted tunnels through miles of solid rock.

While performing these complex and dangerous tasks, workers had to endure broiling summer heat and bitter winter cold, as well as fierce snowstorms. Some workers died of heat exhaustion in desert areas or froze to death in mountain passes. Another threat to the workers came from Native Americans, who resented the invasion of their ancestral land. Members of the Sioux, Cheyenne, Arapaho, and other tribes tried to stop construction by attacking railroad workers, tearing up track, and derailing trains running on the railway. Although Native Americans sometimes slowed down construction, they failed to stop workers from building the railroad through the heart of their homeland.

The cost of the transcontinental railroad was as monumental as the construction, though historians are unsure about the exact price. Estimates of the Central Pacific line range from about $36 million to $51.5 million. One investor, Oakes Ames, attested the Union Pacific line cost about $60 million. The federal government funded the project in what was, at the time, the largest joint venture ever between the federal government and private businesses.

Despite the high cost of the transcontinental railroad, most people believed it was a bargain at any price. In 1862, Henry Wilson, a Massachusetts senator who would later become the nation's 18th vice president, said he did not care how much the railroad cost:

> *I would sink $100,000,000 to build the road and do it most cheerfully, and think I had done a great thing for my country. What are $75,000,000 or $100,000,000 in opening a railroad … that shall connect the people of the Atlantic and Pacific … Nothing!*[3]

Wilson and many other political figures supported the railroad because they believed it was vital to the American dream of expanding the nation westward all the way to the Pacific Ocean.

Westward Expansion

To modern Americans, it is hard to imagine a time when the country did

From Trail to Track

The transcontinental railroad ran 1,776 miles (2,858 km) from Omaha, Nebraska, to Sacramento. It ran west out of Nebraska along the Platte River. After dipping slightly into the northeastern corner of Colorado, it continued across the length of Wyoming. The railroad crossed the Rocky Mountains at the Great Divide Basin in Wyoming. It then cut down through northern Utah and Nevada before crossing the Sierra Nevada into California. The route followed trails that had been used since the mountain men began heading to the Rocky Mountains in the 19th century's first decade. The railroad's general route was known during the 19th century as the Emigrant Road, Oregon Trail, and California Trail. The transcontinental railroad did not strictly follow these older trails, but they used them as guidelines. It crossed or passed over several mountain ranges, spanned countless rivers, and cut through land that would eventually belong to six states. Wyoming, Colorado, and Utah were still just territories when the railroad was being built.

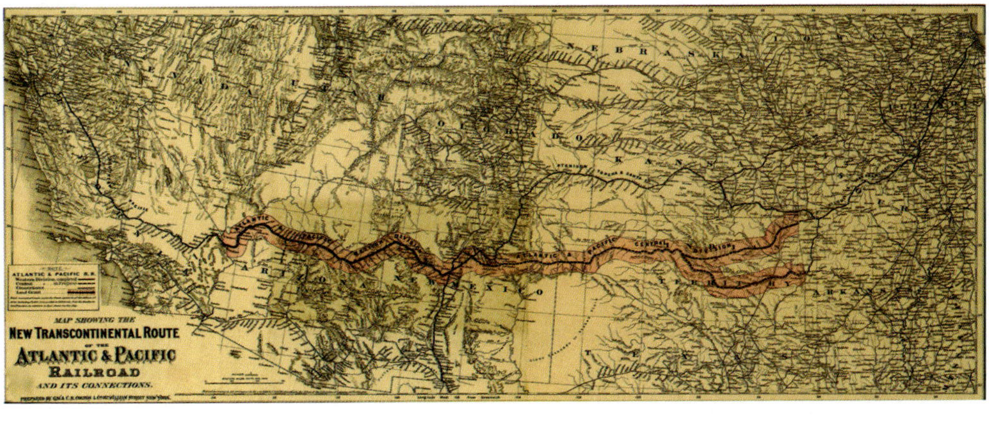

This map shows the size of the transcontinental railroad project in length and the diversity of landforms the railroad had to traverse.

not stretch from coast to coast. However, when the United States was formally recognized as a country in 1783, after winning its freedom from Great Britain in the American Revolution, the nation consisted of 13 colonies along the coast of the Atlantic Ocean. Settlers soon began pushing

In the 1800s, American art romanticized the idea of Manifest Destiny in works such as Emanuel Leutze's Westward the Course of Empire Takes Its Way, *shown here.*

westward in search of new homes, and within a few decades, Americans had become confident that they could extend the boundary of their young, growing nation all the way to the Pacific Ocean. The young nation's

dream of a country stretching from the Atlantic to the Pacific Ocean became known as Manifest Destiny. By the middle of the 19th century, the United States had succeeded in obtaining possession of the vast area of land it wanted from Great Britain, France, Spain, Mexico, and Russia. The United States, however, faced a severe problem in governing the huge new territory it had claimed. The main reason was that it was so difficult and took so long—up to six months—for people to travel and move goods between the nation's eastern and western territories. The transcontinental railroad would solve this transportation problem by providing a quick and reliable way to carry people and goods throughout the nation.

Millions of Americans, both common citizens and high-ranking politicians, believed a rail line would be essential in keeping their rapidly expanding country together. The railroad would help more people move into wilderness areas and create new, productive communities in the huge distance between the settled East and West Coasts. These were seen as important steps in making the middle section and western areas of the nation truly part of the United States.

Chapter One

A SPRAWLING NATION

The route that would become the transcontinental railroad was not wholly the design of railroad employees. Rather, much of it was already explored by Native Americans, the first inhabitants of the land, thousands of years before it became the United States. Bison and other animals also created paths as they followed rivers, such as the Platte, leading them to water and plentiful grass. In the mid-1800s, an estimated 30 to 60 million bison still roamed the Great Plains through which the railroad would be built, though their numbers would soon be greatly reduced.

When European settlers came to North America, they began to head west. In the early years of the United States, fur trappers in search of beavers were the first white explorers to journey to the Rocky Mountains. They were followed by Mormons, who reached the Great Salt Lake Valley, in what is now Utah, in 1847. Other settlers headed West to California and Oregon in search of new homes, hearing stories of the abundance of natural resources—such as California's gold.

No matter the trail, all travelers were in for a long journey. Whether people were riding horses or driving a wagon pulled by a team of horses, mules, or oxen, it took months to travel to the West Coast. Those early travelers faced additional hardships. They experienced violent and unpredictable weather, shortages of food and water, illnesses and injuries, and attacks by thieves and Native Americans. They also faced boredom, as Luzena Wilson described in her account of her trek to California in 1849:

> *Nothing but actual experience will give one an idea of the plodding,*

This 19th-century painting, Pioneers Crossing the Plains of Nebraska, *idealizes the wagon trains that moved across the country. The realities of the experience were much more dangerous.*

unvarying monotony, the [frustrations], the exhaustive energy, the throbs of hope, the depths of despair, through which we lived. Day after day, week after week, we went through the same weary routine of breaking camp at daybreak ... cooking our [small] rations over a fire of sage-brush and scrub-oak; packing up again, coffeepot and camp-kettle; washing our scanty wardrobe in the little streams we crossed; striking camp again at sunset, or later if wood and water were scarce. Tired, dusty, tried in temper, worn out in patience, we had to go over the weary experience tomorrow.[4]

The transcontinental railroad would reduce this incredibly difficult cross-country expedition to just a few days and eliminate many of the hardships and hazards travelers once faced. The new mode of transportation would also speed up the process of settling the huge, sprawling American nation that was growing rapidly. This ancient path, created by Native Americans and wild animals, would soon be home to tracks that would bring in a new modern era of migration, interstate and international trade, and communication. It ensured the United States, a nation whose incredible growth threatened to splinter it, would remain a unified country.

Gazing Westward

After the American Revolution, the United States consisted of a thin strip of 13 states along the coast of the Atlantic Ocean. However, even before the new nation was born, people had begun venturing westward to claim land for new homes and settlements. By the early 1780s, while the American Revolution was still being fought, thousands of people had flocked to the wilderness that would become the states of Tennessee and Kentucky.

The burning desire for land would propel Americans westward until they reached the Pacific Ocean. In 1803, President Thomas Jefferson ensured westward expansion could continue when he arranged the Louisiana Purchase with France. For $15 million, the United States bought a huge expanse of land that France claimed it owned. Running south from the Canadian border to the Gulf of Mexico and west from the Mississippi River to the Rocky Mountains, this new territory doubled the size of the country only two decades after the United States was founded. The Louisiana Purchase included the future states of Arkansas, Iowa, Louisiana, Missouri, South Dakota, Colorado, Minnesota, Montana, North Dakota, Oklahoma, Kansas, and Wyoming.

Jefferson was eager to make the deal because the unknown lands to the west had intrigued him since he was a child. As an adult, Jefferson had a vision that "our rapid multiplication [of U.S. citizens] will expand itself [and] cover the whole northern, if not the southern continent [North and South America] with a people speaking the same language, governed in similar forms [and] by similar laws."[5] The Louisiana Purchase, signed by Jefferson on May 2, 1803, was a giant step forward in making that vision come true.

Another key move Jefferson made to expand the country was to authorize an expedition to explore the North American continent all the way west to the Pacific Ocean. U.S. Army officers Meriwether Lewis and William Clark set out from St. Louis, Missouri, on May 14, 1804, with a party of 33 members. It took them until November of 1805 to reach the Pacific Ocean as they walked, rode horses, and paddled canoes to make the cross-country journey. Their return trip was also slow—they did not reach St. Louis to end the expedition until September 23, 1806.

The reports Lewis and Clark brought

back about the abundant wildlife, towering forests, and rich land they saw during their long journey made many Americans eager to move west and inhabit those areas. The seeds of Manifest Destiny were planted in the American spirit.

Unparalleled Expansion

Fur trappers soon began journeying to the Rocky Mountains to trap beaver. Before the beaver-trapping era ended in the 1830s, the trappers, who became known as mountain men, had helped find new routes west to present-day Oregon and California. The most important discoveries they made were passes over the Rocky Mountains that could be used by settlers with wagons. In the 1830s, people began using these routes to move to the continent's western coast, even though it was not officially part of the United States.

Many settlers went to what was called Oregon Country, an area of the Pacific Northwest that both Great Britain and the United States claimed as their own. They were attracted to that far western area by reports from missionaries who had traveled there to convert Native Americans to Christianity. The missionaries described a land that had plentiful wildlife and rich soil for farming. During this period, the nation's middle section was considered a barren desert unfit for human life because of mistaken accounts from early explorers of the area. Political leaders, such as Missouri senator Thomas Hart Benton, even encouraged Americans to move to Oregon Country because they felt their presence would help the United States win control of the area. "I say to them all, 'Go on!'" Benton said. "The government will follow you, and will give you protection and land!"[6]

Within a few years, so many Americans were living in Oregon Country that Great Britain agreed to surrender most of the disputed territory. On June 18, 1846, a treaty with Great Britain gave the United States a huge area that yielded the future states of Oregon, Washington, and Idaho, as well as parts of Montana and Wyoming.

The acquisition of Oregon Country, however, was just one of three major events that occurred within a few years that helped enlarge the United States. In 1845, the U.S. government annexed the Republic of Texas, a nation that was formed in 1837 after U.S. citizens living there fought against Mexico to win their independence. In 1848, the United States won the Mexican-American War to gain title to land that today includes the states of California, Nevada, Utah, most of Arizona, and parts of Colorado, New Mexico, and Wyoming.

At first, only a trickle of settlers began moving that far west because the journey was long and dangerous and because little was known about the nation's western coast. However, once gold was discovered in the California territory in 1848, there was

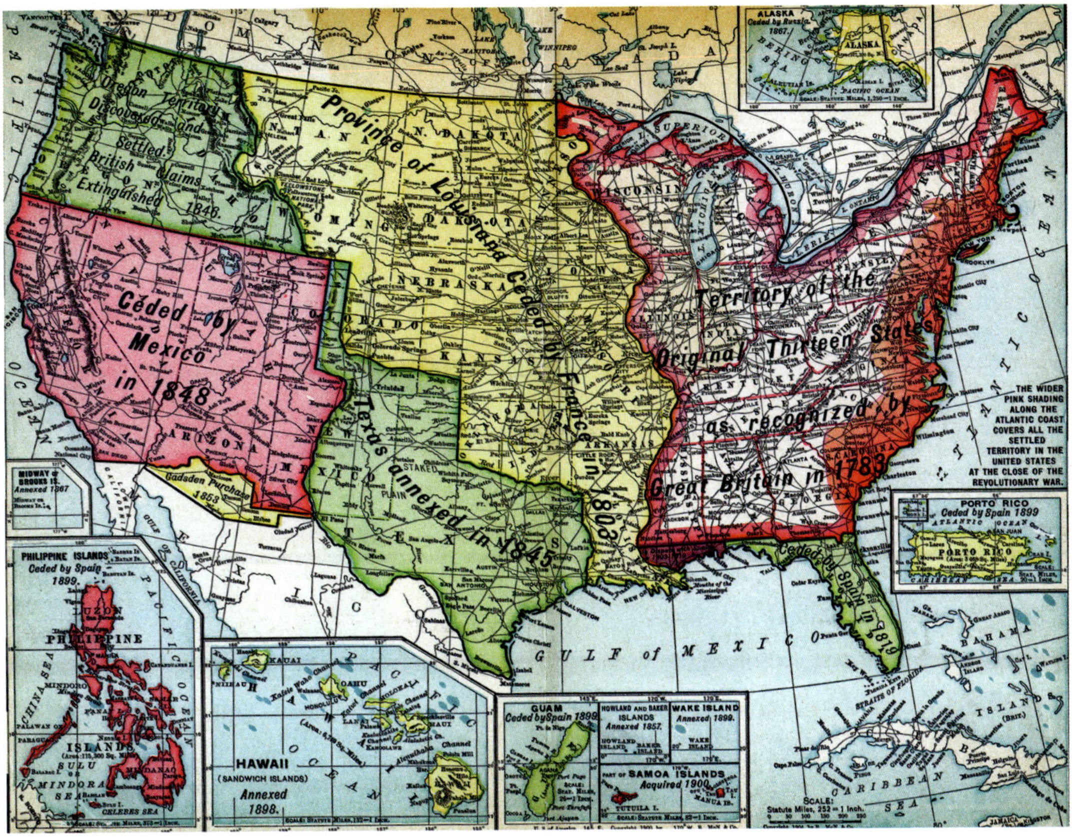

This map shows the explosive rate of American growth in the early and middle 1800s.

a huge migration of gold seekers to the future state. In the decade before the discovery, only a few thousand people had moved to California, but in 1849 alone, some 80,000 prospectors arrived. By 1853, more than 250,000 people had flocked to California to search for gold, farm, or begin other businesses.

The vast expanse of territory that officially became part of the country in just a few years made the United States one of the world's largest nations. Since it had been established in 1783, the United States had experienced exceptional growth as it extended its boundaries westward by thousands of miles in little more than half a century. This unprecedented national growth had long been a concern for some elected officials. As far back as 1817, John C. Calhoun, who in 1825 would become vice president, had declared, "We are greatly, and rapidly—I was about to say fearfully—growing."[7] Calhoun had been worried how the U.S. government could effectively govern such a huge, rapidly growing young nation. His fears began to be realized

"As Solemn as a Funeral"

In his autobiography, J. Henry Brown described his journey to Oregon in 1847 with his grandparents. His grandparents did not seek riches in the new land; they wanted to escape their swampy home in Illinois, which they believed caused them illnesses. Brown's account is a reminder that not only did travelers experience difficulties on the journey, but merely the departure could be heartbreaking for those leaving and those left behind. Separating families knew they might never see each other again because of the great distance and the troubles of travel:

> *Although I was quite young the scene was [permanently] fixed upon my mind. Tears were shed by mother and daughters as they embraced each other for the last time on earth, and the parting kiss was given as the last token of love from the hearts that knew the parting was forever. It was as solemn as a funeral … But the final hour had come, the word was given and the train started on its long, weary six months of travel and toil.*[1]

1. J. Henry Brown, *J. Henry Brown: Autobiography*. Oregon, 1938, PDF. Retrieved from the Library of Congress, www.loc.gov/resource/wpalh3.30020231/?sp=5.

when tens of thousands of settlers began moving to the West Coast.

Connecting the Coasts

California's population increased extremely quickly after the discovery of gold. Soon, that gold became so important to the United States as a source of revenue that the California territory was accepted into the Union as the nation's 31st state in 1850. Along with California, the future states of Oregon and Washington were also growing quickly because so many settlers were heading west.

This rapid expansion created a big problem. It was difficult for the eastern half of the nation to communicate with and travel to the West Coast over such long distances. For example, it is 2,572 miles (4,139 km) from New York City to San Francisco, California. It took four to six months for people and goods to travel that far by wagon or horseback, and the journey was difficult and dangerous. A sea voyage from the East to the West Coast—13,000 miles (20,921 km) around the southern tip of

South America—took much less time but was far more expensive. In addition, the huge area of land between the established eastern states and the West Coast was inhabited by Native Americans. The first inhabitants of the United States had been hostile to newcomers ever since the first white settlers arrived because these settlers stole their land and treated them as inferior beings. As such, it was dangerous to travel through land that Native Americans still held.

These conditions made Californians feel isolated from the rest of the nation. In the mid-1850s, residents of the new state were asking Congress to establish a swift method of overland mail delivery to ease the problem. It took six months by ship for most letters to come from East to West. In 1857, Congress accepted the bid of John Butterfield's Overland Mail Company to start a stagecoach line between St. Louis and San Francisco. The line was able to deliver mail and passengers in a jolting, rocky journey that took between 20 and 25 days to cover a 2,800-mile (4,506 km) route that snaked across the country's midsection.

The company established stations at intervals where drivers could change horses so the stagecoaches could travel quickly. The stagecoaches, sometimes called "swift wagons," covered 5 to 10 miles per hour (8 kph to 16 kph) over flat ground and more than 100 miles (161 km) in a single day. This was an astonishing distance to be able to travel at the time. When the first stagecoach from Butterfield arrived in San Francisco in 1858, it was a time of celebration. The establishment of a solid and dependable stagecoach route meant that California would now really be connected to the rest of America.

Mail delivery was accelerated even more when the Pony Express began delivering letters. In 1860, riders could carry letters in 10 days from Missouri to California. Young men, such as 14-year-old William Cody, who would later become known as Buffalo Bill, rode horses as fast as they could between 190 stations where they changed to fresh mounts. However, riders could only carry a few dozen letters at a time, and it was expensive—$5 for a half ounce, an amount that would be more than $100 today—that most mail still went by stagecoach. Mail couriers had to ride light not just to ensure speedy delivery, but because they sometimes had to escape from attacking Native Americans or outlaws. Cody once said, "Road-agents and Indians infested this country. I never was quite sure when I started out when I should reach my destination, or whether I should never reach it at all."[8]

The Pony Express ceased operation on October 24, 1861, when telegraph lines were connected to the West Coast, which enabled messages to be delivered almost instantaneously. Stagecoach lines still continued taking the bulk of the mail, as well as a few passengers. In addition, large shipping

This wood engraving depicts a Pony Express rider waving his hat at workers erecting the first transcontinental telegraph.

firms such as Wells Fargo and Adams Express were hauling millions of shipments, including postage, passengers, and freight, between the two sides of the nation, even though it took months for the goods and people to reach their destinations.

Just as the invention of the telegraph had miraculously increased the speed of correspondence, a new form of transportation was about to revolutionize transportation of people and products. This new mode of travel was the railroad, and it would soon stretch from coast to coast.

To Preserve the Union

The acquisition of California and Oregon caused Americans to fear that the two halves of the nation might not remain united politically unless a better form of transcontinental transportation could be found. Some people were worried that California or other western states might break away from the United States because they did not truly feel part of the Union due to their physical isolation from the country's political and commercial centers. On May 18, 1849, U.S. Army colonel James Abert wrote a letter to Francis Markoe, a State Department official. Abert, who as a member of the Topographical Engineers had explored the West, noted the problem and offered a solution. Abert said the nation needed to build a railroad across the entire country:

> *The consequences of such a road are immense. They probably involve the integrity of the Union. Unless some easy, cheap, and rapid means of communicating with these distant provinces be accomplished, there is danger, great danger, that they will not constitute parts of our Union.*[9]

Abert's proposal in 1849 was not new. Others had the same idea. It was in 1826 that John Stevens, an early supporter of American railroads, had first demonstrated how a steam engine could be used to pull cars on an experimental railway he built on his estate in Hoboken, New Jersey. In 1830, the first small rail line began operating in the United States; it was a 13-mile (21 km) section of railroad that carried stone from a quarry. The efficiency and speed with which railroads could move people and goods led to a building boom in eastern states.

Not long after seeing the potential for rail travel, companies began building huge rail lines. This got people thinking of a transcontinental railroad. In 1832, Hartwell Carver published an article in the *New York Courier & Enquirer* proposing the idea of a cross-country rail system. That same year, Judge S.W. Dexter of Ann Arbor, Michigan, suggested the idea in an editorial in *Emigrant*, a weekly newspaper for people considering moving west. In 1833, Reverend Samuel Parker, a missionary who had led settlers to Oregon to bring Christianity to Native Americans, claimed, "There would be no difficulty in the way of constructing a railroad from the Atlantic to the Pacific Ocean."[10] The most influential early supporter of a transcontinental railroad was Asa Whitney, a New York merchant. Though not the earliest supporter, it was Whitney who made the first realistic proposal for a continent-spanning railroad.

Asa Whitney's Imperfect Plan

In 1845, Asa Whitney presented a plan to Congress to build a railroad running to the Pacific coast. He said the railroad would start in Prairie du Chien, Wisconsin, after which it would run west toward the Rocky Mountains. It would continue to the mouth of the Columbia River in Oregon, the end point of the westward journey of Lewis and Clark. Whitney estimated the construction cost at $65 million. He claimed, "[It] would bring all our immensely widespread population together as one vast city; the moral and social effects of which must harmonize all together as one family, with but one interest—the general good of all."[11] In addition to creating unity between the eastern and western portions of the nation, Whitney also believed it would benefit the United States economically. A transcontinental railroad was the missing transportation link that would allow businessmen, including Whitney, to easily and cheaply import and export goods to and from China and other countries. At that time, any goods traded between Asia and the United States were transported by ships. The voyages were long, dangerous, and expensive. Many, including Missouri senator Thomas Hart Benton, one of the era's most influential political figures, shared Whitney's view. Benton said such a railroad would ensure that "the rich commerce of Asia will flow through our [nation's]. And where has that commerce ever flowed without carrying wealth and [power] with it?"[12]

Benton, however, was one of the leaders in Congress who rejected Whitney's idea in 1845. He would reject the plan several times over the next few years, as Whitney kept resubmitting his ideas. Benton opposed the plan because he favored a transcontinental railroad that started in St. Louis, which was in his home state of Missouri. Many people also opposed Whitney because of the way he wanted to fund the cross-country railroad. He wanted the government to grant him 60-mile (97 km) strips of land along the length of its route. He would make money to build the railroad by selling the land to settlers in new communities that he was sure would spring up along the railroad line. Whitney claimed land sales would produce enough money to not only pay for the railroad, but also provide funding for schools and other public projects. Many people who supported the idea of a transcontinental railroad were nervous that Whitney was just a crook who was trying to steal land that belonged to all the people of the United States.

Whitney also faced opposition from people who did not believe he had the knowledge to build such a railroad. Whitney had not hired engineers to plan how to build bridges or paths over rivers, ravines, and the Rocky Mountains, and he had not come up with a detailed route for the railroad. An editorial in the *American Railroad Journal* on April 5, 1851, explains this opposition to Whitney's plan:

> *So long as his mission was confined to the matter of arousing the attention of our people to the*

Asa Whitney was an advocate for the transcontinental railroad. His interest in trade with China influenced his push for the transportation route.

Whitney's Appeal

Asa Whitney never got Congress to approve his own plan for a transcontinental railroad. It failed because there were weaknesses in his proposal, including practical considerations of a final route and how to overcome geographic obstacles, such as rivers and mountain passes, and how much he would personally benefit from the project. Despite his political failure, Whitney was engaging when discussing the railroad. In speeches and articles he wrote, he helped make many people support the idea of a transcontinental railroad. In an article printed in many cities on the East Coast, he wrote:

> *If Congress will give me the lands, in a very few months the work shall be commenced, and far sooner than I have dared to hope, it will be completed—when we shall have the whole world … tumbled into our lap—when this vast and now useless waste and wilderness (and it ever must be so, without this road) shall become, not only the thoroughfare of the vast world, but its garden, feeding, clothing, comforting and enlightening millions, who are now starving, homeless, naked, ignorant and oppressed; and who can oppose such a work?*[1]

1. David Haward Bain, *Empire Express: Building the First Transcontinental Railroad*. New York, NY: Penguin Putnam, 1999, pp. 21–22.

> *importance of the proposed work, his success was remarkable. The moment he came to the question of construction his plans failed to receive respectful attention.*[13]

Slow Progress

Although Whitney was not able to get Congress to go along with his plan, his efforts made millions of Americans agree that the nation needed a transcontinental railroad. Even his opponents realized that such a railway would strengthen the nation and help settle its large midsection. For example, Senator Benton, who rejected Whitney's plan, believed the railroad was necessary to achieve Manifest Destiny, a philosophy he fully supported. The phrase "Manifest Destiny" would come to be the defining characteristic of the push to build the transcontinental railroad. The term was first used in an editorial in the *United States Magazine, and Democratic Review* in 1845. John Louis O'Sullivan wrote: "Our manifest destiny [is] to overspread and to possess the whole of the continent which Providence has given us for the development of the great experiment of liberty and federated self-government entrusted to us."[14]

By the early 1850s, most people firmly believed the United States needed a transcontinental railroad to achieve its national goals. The only problems were finding a practical route for the railroad and getting Congress to approve it. It would take nearly another decade to accomplish both tasks and begin work on the project.

Chapter Two

PLOTTING A COURSE ACROSS THE CONTINENT

American history is full of daring pioneers who paved the way for the settlement and expansion of the nation. However, some explorers have slowed down, or even prevented, growth. One such explorer was U.S. Army major and engineer Stephen H. Long. Long was charged with exploring the land between the Mississippi River and the Rocky Mountains in 1819. Secretary of War John C. Calhoun noted in his orders to Long:

> *The object of the expedition is to acquire as thorough and accurate knowledge as may be [possible] of a portion of our country which is daily becoming more interesting but which is yet but imperfectly known. With this in view you will permit nothing worthy of notice to escape your attention.*[15]

Though Long did return with detailed maps that were used for decades, he called the entire area that would become the states of Nebraska and Oklahoma an uninhabitable American desert. Long's description heavily influenced the reluctance of many to expand the United States westward. Several years later, Massachusetts senator Daniel Webster would call the land "vast [and] worthless" in an effort to persuade fellow legislators to not agree to develop the area: "To what use could we ever hope to put these great deserts … What can we ever hope to do with the western coast, a coast of three thousand miles … cheerless, uninviting, and not a harbor on it? What use have we for such a country?"[16]

Even the wonders of Lewis and Clark's account of their journey to the Pacific could not convince Americans that the land west of the Mississippi

River was worthy of consideration. Undeniably, travelers in that direction faced deadly, often insurmountable, and always difficult obstacles. That made a project such as the transcontinental railroad seem unreasonable, at least for a time. Even those who supported the idea did not know if it was possible to build a railroad through the rugged, unknown wilderness. A group of talented and brave explorers, some of whom died in their attempts, eventually found a practical route for the celebrated railroad.

First to Go West

Lewis and Clark were not the first explorers to travel across the entire continent. They reached the Pacific Ocean in 1805, more than a decade after Scottish explorer Sir Alexander Mackenzie had arrived there in 1793, after leading a Canadian group across the continent. The purpose of both expeditions, however, was the same: to find routes to western areas so England and the United States could claim and eventually settle them.

Although the Lewis and Clark expedition was deemed a success, the explorers only saw a small portion of the vast wilderness that lay west of the settled United States. In the next half century, hundreds of individuals and groups would explore the area more fully. What they learned would gradually help the government fill in the huge blank spots that still existed in the most current maps of the western half of the continent.

The people who went west to explore the strange new lands included fur trappers, businessmen, and military officers. Many of them journeyed west for financial gain, commonly in the form of commercial trade or animal fur to sell back east. They were also motivated by another desire: to go where no one but Native Americans had ever gone and discover more about the mysterious West. Jedediah Smith summed up that feeling better than anyone. On August 7, 1826, Smith wrote why he originally headed west from his native Bainbridge, New York:

> *I [had a] strong inclination to visit this unexplored country and unfold those hidden resources of wealth and bring to light those wonders which I … imagined a country so extensive might contain. I must confess that I had at that time a full share of … ambition … I [wanted] to be the first to view a country on which the eyes of a white man had never gazed and to follow the course of rivers that run through a new land.*[17]

In addition to harvesting beaver pelts, mountain men similar to Smith made important discoveries about the West's geography, including routes over the Rocky Mountains and trails to California, which was a Spanish colony at the time. Smith's most important discovery was the South Pass in 1824. That pass, one of the few that went over the Rocky Mountains, would be used in the coming decades by

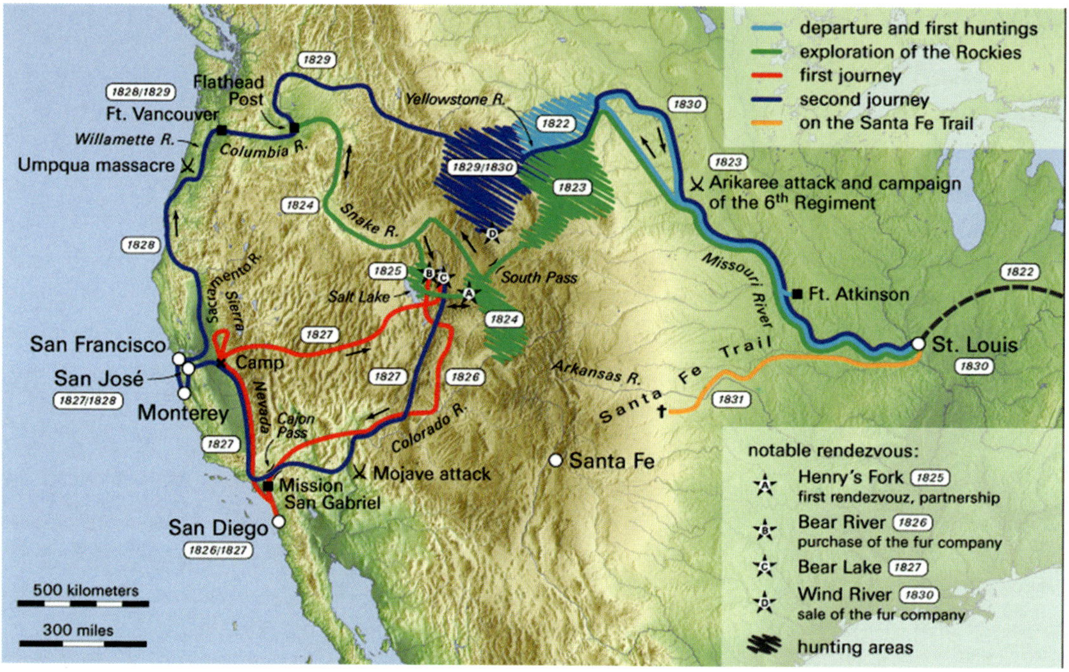

This map shows the expeditions of Jedediah Smith in the early 19th century. Many of his discoveries were useful in the construction of the transcontinental railroad.

hundreds of thousands of settlers traveling by wagon to Oregon and California.

As more and more people moved westward and discovered how rich the land beyond the Rockies was, the federal government began to realize it needed to learn more about that wilderness. In 1838, the U.S. Army created the Corps of Topographical Engineers, a branch of the military whose main duty was to explore and map the continent. The most famous member of this group was John C. Frémont.

Frémont Falters

Between 1842 and 1854, John C. Frémont made many major expeditions into the West. He was nicknamed the "Pathfinder" because he mapped numerous rivers, lakes, deserts, mountains, and even volcanoes, such as Mount St. Helens in Washington. In 1842, Frémont began surveying what became the Oregon Trail as far as the South Pass and explored the Wind River Range of the Rocky Mountains.

Frémont, with the help of his wife, Jessie, wrote a vivid account of his first expedition that was widely read by the general public and helped increase interest in settling the West Coast. Jessie was the daughter of Senator Thomas Hart Benton, who supported western expansion during his three decades in the Senate. In 1848, Benton used his political power to assign his son-in-law to a mission that he believed was vital to realizing his goal of Manifest Destiny: finding a path through the Rocky Mountains for a transcontinental railroad.

This expedition, one of Frémont's latest trips to the West, included 35 men and 120 mules. The group began its trek westward in late 1848. Frémont wanted to find out if there was a passable route over the mountains in winter, which would ensure the future railroad could run year-round. When the expedition reached the Rocky Mountains in Colorado, trappers and Native Americans warned Frémont that bitter winter weather had already descended on the Rocky Mountains

Though Frémont was unable to plot the railroad's route across the Rocky Mountains, he would later use his explorations to attract voters when he ran for president in the 1856 election.

A Corps of Explorers

The U.S. Army Corps of Topographical Engineers played an important role in both exploring the West so it could be settled and mapping out a route for the transcontinental railroad. Historians have been able to uncover some of the reasons why America's history of exploration got started:

> *As [historians have] discovered fairly recently, "Frémont's 1842 expedition was part of an ongoing plan for extensive scientific explorations of the Rocky Mountain Regions," and it was … Joel R. Poinsett (Martin Van Buren's secretary of war at the time) [who] had gone before Congress in 1839 and again in 1840, urging an ambitious program of exploration that would extend "our researches over the Rocky Mountains to the shores of the Pacific Ocean."*[1]

1. Andrew Menard, *Sight Unseen: How Frémont's First Expedition Changed the American Landscape*. Lincoln, NE: University of Nebraska Press, 2012, p. 126.

and would make his journey very dangerous. Frémont ignored their advice. He wrote in his journal:

> *[They] say they have never known the snow so deep in the mountains so early, and that there is every prospect of a severe winter. But this does not deter us. I have my party well prepared and … expect to overcome all obstacles.*[18]

Frémont and his men would pay dearly for his overconfidence. They were trapped in the mountains by the bitter cold and huge amounts of snow. Caught unprepared without snowshoes, the men and mules struggled for days to make any progress forward. Frémont finally decided to turn back, but things got even worse as his men and the mules started becoming sick and dying from the severe cold and lack of food. One of the expedition's members eventually led a rescue party to bring the main group down from the mountains into the small community of Taos, which was then part of the New Mexico Territory. By the time Frémont's expedition reached safety, 10 of its members had already died from cold or starvation. Some reports indicate that the group was so desperate they actually ate one of their dead members. Whether

Frémont Fails Once More

In 1853, when Congress ordered a survey of a route for a transcontinental railroad, Senator Thomas Hart Benton tried to have John C. Frémont, placed in charge of the group that would survey the 38th parallel. When the army turned him down, Benton arranged financing so Frémont could lead a private expedition to find a winter pass over the Rocky Mountains. On September 20, 1853, Frémont set out with a party of 22 men, 10 of them Delaware Native Americans. The cold, snowy winter weather and lack of food defeated Frémont and forced him to turn back. Frémont biographer Tom Chaffin described how harsh the conditions became:

> *By the time the men reached the Wasatch Range … they had eaten a porcupine, a beaver, and most of their horses. As [one member] recalled their grim menu, the horses' "hide was roasted so as to burn the hair and make it crisp, the hoofs and shins were disposed of by regular rotation."*
>
> *In early February [1854], they struck a wagon trail that connected to the Mormon settlements below. That same day, the party experienced the expedition's first and only casualty—Oliver Fuller, who, consumed by frostbite and exposure, died in the saddle. The next day, the party straggled into Parowan [a community in Utah].*[1]

1. Tom Chaffin, *Pathfinder: John Charles Frémont and the Course of American Empire*. New York, NY: Hill and Wang, 2002, p. 395.

this historical legend is true or not, Frémont's mission was a dismal failure.

Finding a suitable railroad path to the West was a difficult task. Another explorer, William H. Warner, had his mission fail soon after Frémont's. A captain with the Corps of Topographical Engineers, Warner tried to find a rail route East from California over the Sierra Nevada. In late September 1849, his expedition was about to cross the southern border of Oregon when the men were attacked by Native Americans. A survivor described Warner's death after he was hit by several arrows: "The Captain's mule turned with him and plunged down the hill; and having been carried about two hundred yards, he fell from the animal dead."[19]

Frémont's failure and the death of Warner and several of his men, however, did not stop the federal government from seeking a route for the transcontinental railroad.

Congressional Orders

After California became a state in 1850 and thousands of settlers began moving into the area, the U.S. government realized that a transcontinental railroad was necessary to provide an effective means of transportation and communication between the two sides of the growing nation. On March 3, 1853, Congress authorized an official survey team to explore the best, cheapest, and safest route for constructing a rail line that would connect the Pacific Ocean to the Mississippi River.

Secretary of War Jefferson Davis was directed to survey possible east-to-west routes along four different parallels, the horizontal lines of latitude on maps that show how far north or south of the equator a location is anywhere on Earth. The northernmost route to be surveyed was between the 47th and 49th parallels from St. Paul, Minnesota, to Puget Sound in Washington. The most central cross-country path was along the 38th parallel from Council Bluffs, Iowa, to San Francisco. The two southern routes were along the 35th parallel from Oklahoma to Los Angeles, California, and along the 32nd parallel from Texas to San Diego, California. A fifth survey, running north to south, was also conducted to find passes through the Sierra Nevada and the Coast Range in California, Oregon, and Washington.

Between all the surveys ordered by Congress, the explorers were going to be hard at work mapping 400,000 square miles of the western half of the continent. They not only had to travel and chart these locations on foot, but they also faced difficulties related to weather, time restrictions, and Native American attacks.

Hazardous Journeys

The route most people believed would be the best was along the 38th parallel. When the surveys were announced, Senator Benton tried to put Frémont in charge of the expedition because it would have closely followed the path of his failed 1848 expedition. Instead, the army chose Captain John William Gunnison, who left Fort Leavenworth in the Kansas Territory on June 23. Gunnison's team was threatened by Ute Native Americans while surveying Cochetopa Pass in southern Colorado and while exploring through the Wasatch Mountains into Utah. On October 18, Gunnison wrote a letter to his wife about the danger from hostile groups in Utah: "There is a war between the Mormons & the Indians & parties of less than a dozen do not dare to travel. We did not know what a risk we have lately been running until coming here."[20]

The threat of Native American attack

became a fatal reality on the morning of October 26, when Paiute Native Americans attacked Gunnison's party while it was camped near a Mormon settlement. Gunnison, his body riddled with arrows, was one of several explorers killed that day. Lieutenant E.G. Beckwith led the survivors into Salt Lake City, Utah, where they spent the winter before resuming their survey along the 38th parallel.

The surviving surveyors were able to continue and eventually finish Gunnison's task, but it took them a long time. Davis did not issue a preliminary report of the findings of the survey teams until 1855. In that year, the government began publishing the complete results, which eventually expanded to be the 12-volume *Reports of Explorations and Surveys, to Ascertain the Most Practicable and Economical Route for a Railroad from the Mississippi River to the Pacific Ocean*. In his preliminary report, Davis praised the work the survey teams had done, even though he admitted they had not answered every possible question about the routes. "We see now, with some precision," Davis wrote, "the nature and extent of the difficulties to be encountered, and, at the same time, the means of [overcoming] them."[21]

Other politicians, however, were not happy with how long the reports took to produce and how incomplete they were. Representative John C. Burch from California was outspoken in his criticism of the reports. Several years after they were published, he claimed they had been nearly useless:

> *The Government had expended hundreds of thousands of dollars in explorations, and elaborate reports thereof had been made and published … yet all this did not demonstrate the [possibility] of a route, nor show the surveys, elevations, profiles, grades or estimates of the cost of constructing the road.*[22]

One of the published reports that was missing critical information was the one Beckwith submitted. His survey was a good one, and it laid out much of the route the Union Pacific would eventually use for its part of the transcontinental railroad. Unfortunately, Beckwith was an artillery officer, not an engineer like Gunnison had been. Beckwith was unable to include cost estimates with his report, so Congress ignored it even though the route was the best. Another route, along the 35th parallel as surveyed by Lieutenant Amiel Weeks Whipple, was also a viable route. However, he made mistakes in estimating the cost of building the railroad. Because the figure he included in the report was twice the amount really needed, Congress rejected his route as well.

The surveys also failed to solve the major problem in building a transcontinental railroad to California, and that was how to get past the towering Sierra Nevada. That task was left up to a civilian named Theodore Dehone Judah, who was nicknamed "Crazy Judah" because of his obsession with building such a railroad.

"Crazy Judah"

There were no railroads in the United States when Theodore Judah was born in 1826, in Bridgeport, Connecticut. From a young age, Judah was interested in the new technology of rail lines. He eventually went to school to become a civil engineer. In his 20s, he worked on the Niagara Gorge Railroad, the Erie Canal, and several other major construction projects across the northeastern United States.

In 1854, Judah moved to California and built a 22-mile (35 km) railroad named the Sacramento Valley line. This was the first railroad west of the Missouri River. It ran from Sacramento to Folsom, the jumping-off spot for prospectors looking for gold in the Sierra Nevada. It was while building this short railroad that Judah, like many other people in California during this period, became obsessed with the idea of a transcontinental railroad. His wife, Anna, once described the passion her husband had for the project: "Everything he did from the time he went to California to the day of his death was for the great continental Pacific railway. It was the burden of his thought day and night."[23]

In 1857, Judah wrote "A Practical Plan for Building the Pacific Railroad," a pamphlet he published and distributed to generate interest in the project. The plan was based on research he had done about building a railroad east from California over the Sierra Nevada. Judah was disappointed in the 1853 surveys the U.S. Army Corps of Topographical Engineers had done because they did not include details important to building a railroad. Judah wrote:

> *It is not considered sufficient to tell [an investor] that somebody has rode over the ground on horseback and pronounced it [usable]. He does not care to be informed that there are 999 different variety and species of plants [along the route].*
>
> *His inquiries are somewhat more to the point. He wishes to know the length of the road. He says, let me see your map and profile … Have you any tunnels … How much masonry … How many bridges … How about timber and fuel?*[24]

Judah put all the appropriate details in his report, and in the next few years, he met with California lawmakers and wealthy California businessmen to increase support for the project. He even went to Washington, D.C., to present his report to congressmen to obtain federal support for his dream railroad. Judah was successful in creating interest in a transcontinental railroad, but there were still important unanswered questions about how to build it. The biggest question was

Theodore Judah's experience lobbying for his Pacific railroad in Washington, D.C., made him realize that he would need to find private investors for such a plan to ever be accomplished.

Preserved in History

The transcontinental railroad would never have been possible without the early explorers who mapped the unknown wilderness through which it eventually ran. Although John C. Frémont did little to map out the railroad's route, his many expeditions into the West and the literature he and his wife, Jessie, wrote about them provided valuable information that helped many

Theodore Judah's monument, shown here, is located in Sacramento. It commemorates his pioneering spirit and work on the transcontinental railroad.

whether a route could be found over the Sierra Nevada where the railroad could be built. This range was massive and troublesome for the new rail line. Without a way to get a train into California, a transcontinental railroad would be impossible. Judah wanted to address this problem himself.

settlers travel there. To honor him, many places are named for him, including counties in Colorado, Idaho, Iowa, and Wyoming; cities in several states, including California; and rivers and mountain peaks.

The town of Gunnison, Colorado, was named in honor of Lieutenant John William Gunnison, who lost his life while leading an expidition in 1853 to map out routes for the rail line. Theodore Judah made one of the key discoveries that made the first transcontinental railroad possible: a path over the Sierra Nevada through Donner Pass. In honor of his contribution, a stone monument was erected in 1931 in a park across from the Southern Pacific Railroad station in Sacramento. The inscription on the monument reads: "That the West may remember Theodore Dehone Judah, pioneer, civil engineer and tireless advocate of a great transcontinental railroad."

Judah's Mission

In 1860, Judah explored a series of routes over the Sierra Nevada with the help of Daniel "Doc" Strong, a drugstore owner in Dutch Flats, a mining town in the foothills of the mountain range. It was difficult to cross the Sierras because they were double-ridged. This means most passable areas consist of two tall peaks and a downward slope to a lower area between them. This was bad for a potential railroad because the tracks would have to climb over two peaks to get across the mountain range. This would make it more expensive, more dangerous, and less practical.

In July 1860, Judah finally settled on a route he believed could truly work for a rail line across the mountains. The path required a railroad company to build over only one ridge. The route was a sloping ascent up the Sierra Nevada between the Yuba and Bear rivers to Donner Pass. From there, the route went downward from the pass and followed the Truckee River out of the mountains into Nevada. It was more practical to build there, and the route was 150 miles (241 km) shorter than one suggested in an 1853 railroad survey.

Donner Pass was infamous as the spot where settlers traveling to California became trapped by heavy snow during the winter of 1846 to 1847. More than a dozen people died from cold and starvation before the group was rescued. There were even reports that survivors were forced to eat those who had died just to stay alive. The Donner Pass, which had been a grim reminder of the dangers of travel, now became the most important section of the future route of the transcontinental railroad.

On November 10, 1860, Judah printed another pamphlet. In it, he boasted he had finally found a reasonable and cost-effective way to cross the Sierra Nevada. His choice of a route helped Judah obtain solid financial support from some of California's richest and most influential businessmen and leaders, collectively known as the Big Four. Judah's efforts resulted in the creation of the Central Pacific Railroad on April 30, 1861.

Armed with a viable route over the Sierras and a corporation ready to build the railroad, Judah headed back to the nation's capital to lobby federal support for the railroad he envisioned. In a little more than a year, the federal government would finally approve a transcontinental railroad.

Chapter Three

A WAY TO PRESERVE THE UNION

The years leading up to the American Civil War were filled with tension. In the U.S. Congress, that tension affected legislation and policy, whether related to slavery or not. This strain impacted the plans for the transcontinental railroad as well. Perhaps as difficult as finding a reasonable route across the country was deciding where in the East the railroad would begin. Both the North and South knew the railroad meant economic benefits for the region through which it would run. Naturally, government officials from northern and southern states hoped the route would pass through their region. Multiple reports and surveys were produced to prove that one direction was better than another. However, these reports were biased and compromises were nearly impossible to reach. Continual disagreement meant the railroad construction could not commence.

In 1858, Abraham Lincoln proclaimed that if Americans could not work together, the country would fall. Theodore Judah also regretted that political rivalries were impeding the railroad: "No one doubts that [the federal government] ought to insure the construction of this Railroad, but [Congress] is the house divided against itself."[25]

Everyone agreed that the railroad was necessary—Judah convinced them of this. Congressional representatives believed it would improve the prospects of the nation, but consensus regarding the plans would prove unattainable for a time. It was impossible for a railroad company—or even several—to build the track without federal assistance. Such a project depended on the federal government to grant money and land. However, with the government in political gridlock, Judah feared for his plans. It would take an act of war—the Civil War—to tear the nation apart for construction of the railway to begin.

Divided Communities

The political fighting over the transcontinental railroad even extended to the leaders who were chosen to make the 1853 surveys. Missouri senator Thomas Hart Benton wanted a railroad that began in St. Louis and followed the route that his son-in-law, John C. Frémont, had disastrously tried to explore in 1848. Illinois senator Stephen A. Douglas, meanwhile, was able to get former army officer Isaac I. Stevens assigned to survey the route he favored, the northernmost one, which ran between the 47th and 49th parallels and started in Wisconsin.

Stevens himself had a major interest in the northern route. He had just resigned from the military so he could become governor of the new Washington Territory, which would benefit greatly if Congress chose the route he was going to explore. The report Stevens submitted to Congress praised the northern route, and he claimed there would be no problem getting through the mountains in that region, even though they were part of the Rocky Mountains. Naturalist George Suckley, who accompanied Stevens on the expedition, disagreed. He even wrote that building a railroad through the northern mountains made as little sense as trying to build a bridge over the Himalayas in Asia—the tallest mountain range in the world.

Secretary of War Jefferson Davis was actually happy to learn of the criticism of a northern route. A southerner born in Kentucky, Davis tried, but failed, to persuade Congress to accept the southernmost 35th parallel route. Davis was so firm in opposing a northern route that other southern congressmen, such as Zedekiah Kidwell of Virginia, criticized him. They said Davis was actually harming the South by not being willing to compromise on a route to ensure that a transcontinental railroad that would benefit the entire nation, including the South, could be built.

In 1857, when Davis was elected as a senator from Mississippi, he continued to support the southern route. In a fiery Senate speech in 1858, Davis responded to people who criticized his persistence: "If the section of which I am a citizen has the best route, I ask who that looks to the interest of the country has a right to deny it the road?"[26] Many people, however, believed he backed that route because it would help the South economically. Although the congressional battle centered on the ongoing fight between North and South, it also divided communities in both sections of the nation. For example, the southern cities of Memphis, Tennessee; New Orleans, Louisiana; and Vicksburg, Virginia, all fought to host the eastern end of the transcontinental railroad. This led congressmen to favor one route over another because it might benefit a city within their district. The inability of Congress to compromise on a route finally ended in 1861 when the nation was engaged in the Civil War.

Jefferson Davis became president of the Confederate States of America when the South seceded from the United States.

An Obstacle Removed

The bitter feelings between the North and South intensified during the 1850s. It peaked on November 8, 1860, when Abraham Lincoln was elected president of the United States. Lincoln was the first U.S. president from the Republican Party, which was founded in 1854 as an antislavery political organization. Fearing that a Republican president would bring an end to slavery in America, southern states began seceding from the Union and formed the Confederate States of America. On April 12, 1861, the Confederate army attacked Fort Sumter in South Carolina in the first battle of the American Civil War.

Although the Civil War was a bloody, terrible period in U.S. history, it created an opportunity for Congress to approve a transcontinental railroad. Many felt that such a railroad was more vital than ever to ensure that California and other western states would continue to support the Union. In addition, it would now be easier for members of Congress to agree on a route for the railroad because southern politicians, such as Jefferson Davis, were no longer around to argue over where it should begin. Dozens of southerners had resigned from Congress to side with the Confederacy. Among them was Davis, who on February 18, 1861, became president of the Confederate States of America.

Another important factor was that President Lincoln and the Republicans, who now had a majority in Congress, supported the railroad. Republicans, in both 1856 and 1860, had included in their national party platform the statement that "a railroad to the Pacific Ocean, by the most central and practical route, is ... demanded by ... the whole country, and that the federal government ought to [give] immediate and efficient aid in its construction."[27]

The new, more favorable attitude toward a transcontinental railroad led Central Pacific officials to send Judah back to Washington in 1861. In written instructions, the officials told him he was being sent "for the purpose of [getting grants] of land and U.S. Bonds from Government, to aid in the construction of this Road."[28] It would take Judah nearly a year to perform this task.

Congress Finally Acts

Judah left California on October 11, 1861, and arrived in Washington, D.C., in late November after a sea voyage. The railroad he wanted to build would cut that same journey from about six weeks to just about seven days. One of his traveling companions was Aaron Sargent, a journalist who had been elected to the U.S. House of Representatives. Sargent was assigned to the House Pacific Railroad Committee. Judah wrote that Sargent's new position on the committee greatly helped him fulfill his task:

> *[Sargent's position] proved an act of great benefit to our future interests, as well as to the State of California, for Mr. Sargent, having no other committee duties to occupy his attention,*

took hold of the Pacific Railroad and devoted his time and energies almost exclusively to that subject.[29]

Even before Judah arrived, Congress had decided to introduce new legislation to build a transcontinental railroad. Because of that, Judah's Central Pacific was not the only railroad company that sent representatives to submit bids to Congress for the right to build it. One of the biggest challengers to the California concern was the Mississippi and Missouri Railroad, which had built a line across Iowa from the Mississippi River to the Missouri River and had dreams of extending it all the way to the Rocky Mountains.

Realizing that he faced tough competition, Judah began talking to as many politicians as he could to win their support for a transcontinental railroad and to make them believe the Central Pacific was best suited to build it. California representative John C. Burch said Judah did an admirable job in winning lawmakers to his side: "His knowledge of his subject was so thorough, his manners so gentle … his conversation on the subject so entertaining that few resisted his appeals."[30]

Judah so impressed the congressmen and senators he met that they gave him influential positions in both the House and Senate special committees for legislation on the proposed railroad. He provided them with detailed

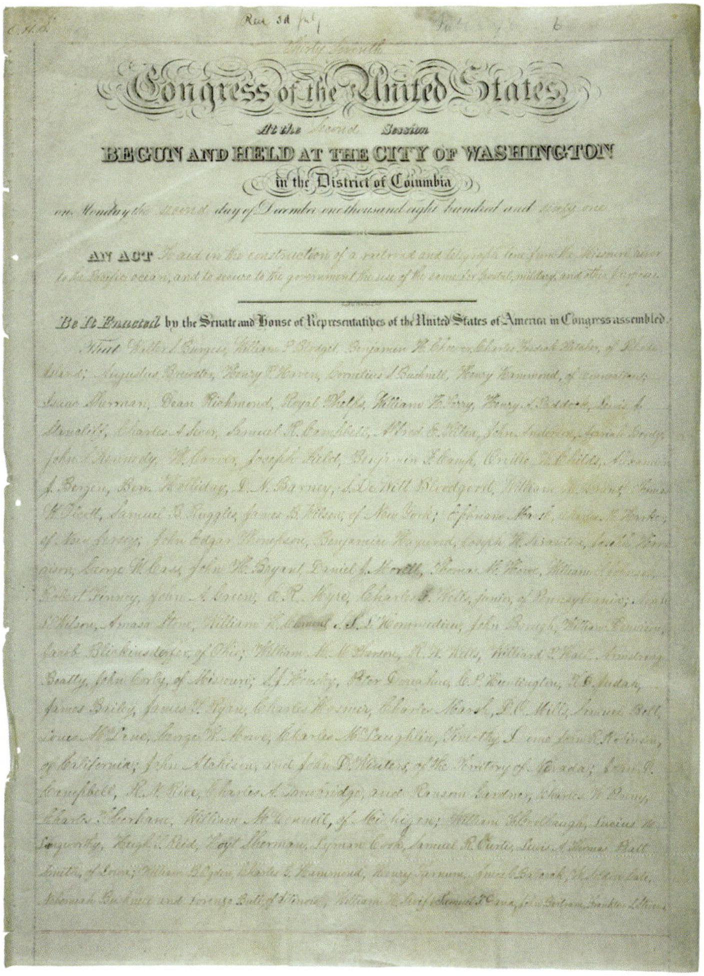

Congress of the United States
At the Second Session
BEGUN AND HELD AT THE CITY OF WASHINGTON
in the District of Columbia
on Monday the second day of December one thousand eight hundred and sixty one

AN ACT To aid in the construction of a railroad and telegraph line from the Missouri river to the Pacific ocean, and to secure to the government the use of the same for postal, military, and other purposes.

Be It Enacted by the Senate and House of Representatives of the United States of America in Congress assembled, [illegible]

The Pacific Railway Act of 1862, shown here, helped make the dream of a transcontinental railroad a reality.

Judah and the Big Four

The top officials of the Central Pacific were named the Big Four because they were among the nation's richest and most powerful rail investors. They were Collis P. Huntington, Mark Hopkins, Leland Stanford, and Charles Crocker. All four became wealthy enough to invest in the railroad through different business enterprises. Stanford, for example, made some money through investments in gold mines, but his main business was running a wholesale retail company. He also helped found the California Party, and he was elected California's first Republican governor, serving from 1862 to 1863. Charles Crocker, another Republican Party leader who once served as a state legislator, was also a merchant, while Huntington and Hopkins owned a company that sold mining equipment. Historians have examined how Theodore Judah brought these powerful men together. The engineer convinced them to join the project by telling them the railroad would be a wise investment: "You are tradesmen here in Sacramento city, your property and your business is here—help me [and] I'll make you the Central Pacific railroad company and [it] will make your fortune in trades, etc. etc."[1]

1. Stephen A. Ambrose, *Nothing Like It in the World: The Men Who Built the Transcontinental Railroad 1863–1869*. New York, NY: Simon & Schuster, 2000. PDF e-book.

Leland Stanford (top left), Charles Crocker (top right), Mark Hopkins (bottom left), and Collis P. Huntington (bottom right), known as the Big Four, were among the earliest—and wealthiest—investors in Theodore Judah's railroad company. They played an important role in making the transcontinental railroad a reality.

information about possible routes, construction requirements, and the estimated cost of building the railroad. Congressmen used Judah's expertise to draft the Pacific Railway Act of 1862. It was the first act of its kind.

After years of political bickering, representatives and senators had finally reached agreement on a bill to build a transcontinental railroad. The main reason they acted was the fear that western states, such as California, might secede from the Union as southern states had. Congressmen firmly believed this new transportation system was a way to strengthen ties with western states and

bring them closer to the Union. California's desire to be part of the Union had been expressed by Chief Justice Stephen J. Field of the California Supreme Court just a few months before. On October 24, 1861, after telegraph lines had finally been connected in Sacramento, Field told President Lincoln in the first telegram sent across the continent that "the people of California ... believe that it will be the means of strengthening the attachment which binds both the East and West of the Union, and they desire ... to express their loyalty to the Union."[31]

Lincoln supported the Railway Act because he supported westward expansion and believed the railroad would solidify ties with the West. The Senate passed the act 35 to 5, and Lincoln signed it into law on July 1, 1862. The bill was not only historic because it authorized a transcontinental railroad, but also because of the unique partnership it created between the federal government and private business.

Partnership to Build

Union general William Tecumseh Sherman, who became famous for destroying much of Georgia during the war, began his military career in the West. While serving there, he wrote to his brother John, a congressman from Ohio, about the need for a transcontinental railroad. Sherman said the project was necessary but incredibly huge. He called it "a work of giants, and Uncle Sam is the only giant I know who can [handle] the subject."[32]

Before 1862, the federal government had wanted private railroad companies to build the historic railroad without its help. However, amid the struggle to unify a nation engaged in a civil war, the railway took on great importance. Lincoln realized the government had to assist the railroad companies to get the project done. He also felt the help had to be limited to financial aid because of the war. Lincoln said, "The National Government has its hands full carrying on the war. Private [businesses] must build the Pacific Railroad, and all the government can do is aid, even admitting its construction is a political as well as a military necessity."[33]

The Pacific Railway Act created two forms of federal aid: government loans and federal land. The government guaranteed railroads a set amount of money for each mile of track laid, ranging from $16,000 in flat plains to $48,000 in the mountains, where it was much more expensive to lay track. In addition to railroad tracks, the government also wanted the companies to build a telegraph system along the route to increase telegraph communication between the eastern and western sections of the nation. The government provided the funding in the form of low-interest loans that had to be repaid within 30 years. In addition, the railroad companies would receive 6,400 acres (2,590 ha) of public land in 10 sections along the railroad line for every mile of track each company built. The railroads could then sell the land to settlers to get more money to cover construction costs. In theory, this would create profits.

Once construction began, however, railroad executives discovered it cost them much more to build each mile than they had calculated. Charles Crocker, one of the four main investors in the Central Pacific, complained after just a few months that the railroad was running out of money because construction was so expensive:

> *I would have been glad, when we had 30 miles of road built, to have got a clean shirt and [freedom] from my debts. I owed everybody that would trust me, and would have been glad to have them forgive my debts and taken everything I had, even the furniture of*

A Fateful Meeting

Abraham Lincoln had been interested in a transcontinental railroad even before he became president. His interest was heightened by a meeting with Grenville M. Dodge, an engineer for the Mississippi and Missouri Railroad. After Dodge helped build the line across Iowa in the 1850s, he explored extending the route to the Rocky Mountains. After meeting Lincoln by chance, the future president was so impressed with Dodge's knowledge that he sought to learn as much as he could about such a railroad. Dodge later recorded how the fateful meeting took place. He wrote:

> *During the explorations, in 1856 or 1857, I happened to return to Council Bluffs [Iowa], where Mr. Lincoln chanced to be on business. It was then quite an event for an exploring party to reach [this far West]. After dinner, while I was sitting on the stoop of the [hotel], Mr. Lincoln came and sat down beside me and, in his kindly way and manner, was soon drawing from me all I knew of the country west, and the result of my surveys. The secrets that were to go to my employers he got.*[1]

1. Quoted in Randall Parrish, *The Great Plains: The Romance of Western American Exploration, Warfare, and Settlement, 1527–1870*. Chicago, IL: A. C. McClurg & Co., 2007, p. 328.

> *my family, and to have gone into the world and started anew.*[34]

In 1864, when railroad officials went back to Washington, D.C., to seek more funding, Congress amended the Railway Act to double the land grants for each company to 12,800 acres (5,180 ha). In all, the federal government gave railroad companies 33 million free acres (13 million ha) of land, which they could later sell to increase their profits from building the railroad.

Picking the Eastern Point

Sacramento was already widely accepted as the western end of the transcontinental railroad. One of the most difficult decisions left to make was to select a site for the historic line's eastern starting point. This decision was complicated by the fact that communities in many northern states were waging a political battle for that honor.

One requirement for the eastern end of the railroad was that the chosen city had to be connected to other railroad lines so that the finished railway would be capable of carrying people and goods across the continent. Many people favored St. Louis, but it was ruled out because it was too close to the intense fighting of the Civil War. A northerly route through Minnesota was considered, but congressmen rejected it because of ongoing battles in the region between settlers and Sioux Native Americans. Omaha, Nebraska, also seemed a good choice because it was on the western side of the Missouri River and at the entrance of the Platte River valley—a viable path to the Rocky Mountains. Another possibility was Council Bluffs, Iowa. Located only a few miles east of Omaha, on the other side of the Missouri River, it was also a major city.

The competition was so fierce that Congress decided to let the president make the final decision. Lincoln talked to many railroad experts before finally making his choice in 1863. The two people who influenced him the most were Grenville Dodge and Thomas C. Durant, who were both connected to the Mississippi and Missouri Railroad. Dodge was an engineer who had mapped a possible route for the railroad west to the Rocky Mountains, while Durant was one of the company's top officials.

Lincoln met with both in 1863 before making his decision. Durant was the most persuasive in telling the president to choose Omaha because it was the most logical. Lincoln agreed with him, even though he feared people would believe he chose it because he owned land that would become more valuable if a railroad was built from Omaha. He told Durant, "I got a quarter-section of land right there and if I [build] it there, they will say that I have done it to benefit my land. But I will fix it there anyhow."[35]

Durant would do more than help decide the eastern end of the transcontinental railroad. He would become the most important official of the Union Pacific Railroad, which the Pacific Railway Act of 1862 created to help the Central Pacific build the line. Congress did this because it believed the task of building a railroad across the country was too big a job for just one company. It ordered the Union Pacific to build eastward from Omaha and the Central Pacific to build westward from Sacramento.

Producing the Union Pacific Railroad

When Lincoln signed the Pacific Railway Act, the Union Pacific Railroad was not much more than a name on a piece of paper. The law created a Board of Commissioners of the Union Pacific Railroad and Telegraph Company to create the new corporation. The board had 158 members, including some chosen by the federal government to represent the government's interests in the railroad. Congress filled out the rest of the board with political and business leaders from a number of states and territories in the Union.

The board members gathered in Chicago, Illinois, on September 2, 1862, for the first official meeting of the Union

Pacific Railroad. They elected officers and agreed on how to sell bonds to raise the vast sums of money they would need to begin construction of the railroad. The money was needed because the Union Pacific and Central Pacific railroads had to actually complete each required mile of track before they could receive federal loans or land as compensation.

Thomas C. Durant operated the Union Pacific and generated a great profit—for himself. This eventually resulted in a major scandal.

William B. Ogden was elected president of Union Pacific. However, the importance of his position was surpassed by Thomas C. Durant, who became the Union Pacific's vice president and general manager in 1863. In this dual role, Durant helped raise money to pay for construction and directed building of the railroad. He also used his influence with Lincoln and Congress to ensure that the project received federal help when it needed it, such as protection by the U.S. Army when Native Americans attacked work crews.

Race to the End

Though the new legislation chose Ogden, Utah, as the end point for the Union Pacific line coming west from Omaha, the initial meeting point for the two lines was Promontory Summit, Utah. However, construction of the transcontinental railroad became a race for riches because the government allowed the two railroads to compete to see which one could lay the most track. The Union Pacific and the Central Pacific could improve their profits if they laid tracks faster than their competitor, and this created an intense rivalry.

It was not just money on the line for the two railroads. There were incentives, such as coal mines and other natural resources, along the designated route. The first railroad to lay track there could claim them as part of the land granted them through the Pacific Railway Act. Moreover, the company that reached Salt Lake City, Utah, first could claim a large population of Mormons as eager passengers ready to pay for rail service. In their haste for riches, the Central Pacific and Union Pacific demanded a lot from their workers. They accepted poor work at times, as it meant more track was laid faster. The competition added to the drama of the construction of the first railroad to span the continent.

Chapter Four

THE UNION PACIFIC HEADS WEST

The Union Pacific Railroad laid 1,086 miles (1,748 km) of track west from Omaha on its way to connect with the Central Pacific. This distance was almost 400 miles (644 km) more than the Central Pacific. While the Union Pacific's route had fewer geographical obstacles than the Central Pacific's route, it began construction months later than the Central Pacific.

Influential men gave the Union Pacific the push it needed to succeed. One of these leaders was Grenville M. Dodge. Dodge was the surveyor hired by Union Pacific operational leader Thomas C. Durant. Dodge had to plot a rail course to the Rocky Mountains. Dodge's exploratory trips convinced him a railroad that traversed the country was possible. Durant, in turn, was convinced that he needed the brilliant man to serve as his chief engineer. In 1866, Dodge—now a decorated general who had fought in the Civil War—resigned from the army and signed on to work for the Union Pacific as chief engineer. His main responsibilities were to examine terrain and design the Union Pacific's route across, over, or through it.

By the time Dodge took the helm, the Union Pacific had already begun laying track along the route that he had recommended. The first 600 miles (966 km) held few physical challenges as they took the railroad through the Platte River valley. In front of them, however, were the foreboding Black Hills, and then the equally challenging Rocky Mountains. Dodge himself found the pass through the Black Hills, and military expeditions had discovered a pass through the Rocky Mountains. There was nothing on the path to stop the Union Pacific.

At the beginning of the Union Pacific's journey west, however, several frustrating challenges unrelated to geographical limitations severely

Grenville M. Dodge, shown here, was a gifted engineer and an esteemed military leader who worked under Union general Ulysses S. Grant.

slowed the railroad's progress. Just one of those barriers was enough to halt the project, and the railroad faced several. Nevertheless, each difficulty was resolved, ensuring that the Union Pacific could begin its race toward the Central Pacific line.

Major Obstacles for the Union Pacific

When the Confederate States of America surrendered to end the American Civil War on April 9, 1865, the Union Pacific had still not built any track. It finally spiked its first rail into the ground two months later on July 10 and began inching westward. Progress was initially slow. In October, General William Tecumseh Sherman and Thomas C. Durant arrived in Omaha to inspect the first 15 miles (24 km) of track. The 45-year-old Sherman said, "I might live to see the day, but can scarcely expect it at my age, when the two oceans will be connected by a complete Pacific railroad."[36] The sarcastic comment by the Civil War hero was an insult to Durant for the slow pace of work on the project.

Although Durant and other executives had done a poor job of getting the railroad underway, they had been slowed by legitimate problems. One was a lack of manpower because potential workers were fighting in the Civil War. In an era without motorized equipment to do the work, thousands of workers were required to haul supplies, level a railroad bed over rough ground, build bridges, and set in place iron rails that each weighed 700 pounds (318 kg). These rails were secured with iron spikes driven into the ground and long blocks of wood, which were called ties. The lack of manpower vanished when the war ended. Suddenly, tens of thousands of soldiers from the North and South, as well as newly arrived immigrants and freed slaves, were available to power the biggest construction project in the nation's history.

A second major problem was a lack of money. Under the Pacific Railway Act of 1862, the 2 railroads had to build 40 miles (64 km) of track before the government would give them the federal loans and land grants for doing the work. The government required that the work be done first to make sure the railroads were actually capable of building hundreds of miles of track. The Union Pacific, however, struggled to raise the $1 million it needed to build the first 40 miles of track. Most businessmen and banks had invested their money in war-related enterprises that returned huge profits, such as manufacturing uniforms and weapons.

Oakes and Oliver Ames, two brothers who had become wealthy selling shovels to California gold miners, helped the Union Pacific in 1865. Oakes, a U.S. representative from Massachusetts, became involved in the railroad after he met with Lincoln in 1865. Lincoln was worried about the Union Pacific's financial problems because it endangered the entire transcontinental railroad project. "Ames, you take hold of this," the president told Oakes. "The road must be built, and you are the man to do it. Take hold of it yourself."[37] Oakes and his brother bought $1 million worth of stock in the Union Pacific and loaned it $600,000 so it could start laying track.

The third problem facing the Union Pacific was perhaps its greatest. Its route ran through the Great Plains, which Native Americans inhabited. The increasing number of white settlers traveling through their homeland was a source of anger and resentment. In 1865, General John Pope was in charge of army units in the area. He warned the federal government of the threat of violence from Native Americans:

> *There is not a tribe of Indians on the great plains or in the mountain regions east of Nevada and Idaho … which is not now warring on the whites … The first demand of the Indian is that the white man shall not come into his*

country, shall not kill or [drive] off the game upon which his [survival] depends, and shall not dispossess him of his lands.[38]

One of the targets of this Native American hostility was the Union Pacific Railroad. During the construction of the railroad, there were countless skirmishes between tribes and workers.

Native Americans Take a Stand

For thousands of years, the Cheyenne, Arapaho, Kiowa, Comanche, and Sioux lived on the vast Great Plains, where they hunted bison and other large animals to survive. To them, wagon trains and other travelers crossing their homeland bound for western areas such as California and Oregon were invaders who threatened their way of life. The Native Americans hated the transcontinental railroad because they realized it would eventually bring more whites and bring the destruction of their ancient home.

Native Americans tried to stop it by stealing the railroad's horses and mules and sometimes even attacking work crews. Teams of surveyors plotting the final route were especially vulnerable, because they worked far from the main work crews and rarely had soldiers to protect them. As the Union Pacific gradually laid more miles of track, Native Americans tried to stop the trains running on them.

The Native Americans were smart in their attacks. They tore up rails so trains would crash and then they would attack and even kill the workers and passengers. One such incident took place in 1867, near Walnut Creek in the Nebraska Territory. Porcupine, a Cheyenne warrior, explained what happened:

We said among ourselves: "Now the white people have taken all we had and have made us poor and we ought to do something. In these big wagons [trains] that go on this metal road [rails], there must be things that are valuable … If would could throw these wagons off the iron they run on and break them open, we should find out what was in them … We got a big stick, and just before sundown one day tied it to the rails and sat down to watch and see what would happen.[39]

A small handcart used by construction crews was riding along the rails and hit the stick. The vehicle was thrown off the rails, and the Native Americans killed several men who had been riding it. They then tore up the track and derailed a freight train. They killed some of the crewmen and looted the freight cars before burning them. The only survivor was William Thompson, who had been left for dead after the handcart crashed. He managed to crawl away after the freight train was derailed.

The situation became so bad that Samuel Reed, a construction leader, wrote Durant to tell him workers were "very timid and at the first appearance of Indians would all leave the work."[40] The federal government stepped in to solve the problem. In the summer of 1867, General Sherman met with tribal leaders to figure out a treaty. The government wanted the Sioux to remain north of the Platte River and the other groups south of the Arkansas River. Sherman explained to them, "This would leave for our people exclusively the use of the wide belt, east and west, between the Platte and Arkansas, in which lie the two great railroads, and over which passes the bulk of travel to the [West]."[41]

In October 1867, the Cheyenne, Arapaho, Kiowa, and Comanche signed three agreements known as the Treaty of Medicine Lodge. In return for the land it sought, the United States promised the groups they could keep most of modern-day Oklahoma. The Sioux signed another treaty giving them all of modern-day South Dakota,

Many Native Americans were outraged at the railroad cutting across their homeland. They tried to fight off construction crews and sabotage tracks.

Dodge's Discovery

Grenville M. Dodge realized that Native Americans were an obstacle to the construction of the Union Pacific line. Yet it was while he fought Native Americans in 1865, as a general in the U.S. Army, that he discovered a pass through the Black Hills for the railroad. Dodge explained how this happened:

> *About noon [on September 22, 1865], in the valley of a tributary of Crow Creek, we discovered Indians, who, at the same time discovered us … I saw our danger and took means immediately to reach [a nearby] ridge and try to head them off, and follow it to where the cavalry could see our signals. We dismounted and started down the ridge, holding the Indians at bay, when they came too near, with our [rifles]. It was nearly night when the troops saw our smoke-signals of danger and came to our relief; and in going to [them] we followed this ridge out until I discovered it led down to the plains without a break. I then said to my guide that if we saved our scalps I believed we had found the crossing of the Black Hills—and over this ridge … the wonderful line over the mountains was built.*[1]

1. Grenville Mellen Dodge, *Romantic Realities: The Story of the Building of the Pacific Roads, as Told by the Engineer Whose Genius Found a Pathway Over the Mountains*. Omaha, NE: J. S. Tebbets, 1889, p. 10.

as well as much of North Dakota and Nebraska west of the Missouri River. The government also promised it would give them food, schools, and other aid. In the next three decades, however, whites moved into the lands that the government had promised to the Native Americans.

Although the treaties eventually reduced the attacks, the Union Pacific still faced threats from small bands of Native American warriors. The U.S. Army began protecting workers with 5,000 soldiers who patrolled the railroad lines. Because the Medicine Lodge Treaty would not be signed for 2 more years, the Union Pacific had laid only 40 miles (64 km) of track by the end of 1865. Though progress was slow, the Union Pacific had reached the minimum required to begin receiving federal loans and land from the government.

Construction Commences

In 1866, the Union Pacific finally started racing westward as its crews set down 266 miles (428 km) of iron rails. This was possible because it had resolved two of its three major problems—a lack of workers and a lack of money—and the government was working on reducing the threat of Native American attacks. The Union Pacific was also assisted when Durant hired several men who brought military precision to the complex construction project.

The most important arrival was Dodge. During the Civil War, he had repaired southern railroads so the U.S. Army could use them to move troops and supplies. When the war ended, Dodge was sent West to lead army units in subduing Native Americans on the Great Plains.

Dodge was still interested in building a railroad across the continent. While patrolling the area, he would explore possible routes. In September 1865, he found a pass through the steep Black Hills that was suitable for a train. It was the first time anyone had discovered a train route through the Black Hills, and Dodge later used it for Union Pacific's final route. He named this passage in the mountain range Sherman Pass, after General William Sherman, his superior officer when he was a Civil War soldier.

Durant had worked with Dodge on the Missouri and Mississippi Railroad. He respected his knowledge and experience. In February 1866, he tried to hire him for the Union Pacific. Dodge refused, but he did send Durant a telegram explaining what he should look for in a chief engineer:

> *Let me impress upon you the importance of commencing the years work by placing at Omaha a chief in whom you have confidence, who in all things you will support and who you can hold responsible that your orders are carried out—and who all connected with the road will know they must obey.*[42]

Durant found two men who would help boost the pace of construction: John "Jack" Casement, a former Civil War general, and his brother Daniel. The Casement brothers were tough, no-nonsense bosses who demanded total obedience from workers and always got it. "General Jack," as he was soon called by workers, was an especially imposing figure, even though he was only 5 feet, 4 inches (163 cm) tall. Durant still wanted Dodge on the project, however. Dodge finally resigned from the army on May 6, 1866, and became Union Pacific's chief engineer—on the condition that he be given complete control of its construction.

A Massive Workforce

Dodge and the Casement brothers were able to coordinate workers in the many complicated tasks of building a railroad, which all had to be accomplished by pure physical strength. The

How to Build a Railroad

The process of laying rail lines, especially lines that are extremely long, was difficult in the 19th century. Journalist William Abraham Bell described the complicated act of constructing the transcontinental railroad:

> *A light car, drawn by a single horse, gallops up to the front [of the track] with its load of rails. Two men seize the end of a rail and start forward, the rest of the gang taking hold by twos, until it is clear of the car. They come forward at a run. At the word of command the rail is dropped in its place, right side up with care, while the same process goes on at the other side of the car. Less than thirty seconds to a rail for each gang, and so four rails go down to the minute … The moment the car is empty it is tipped over on the side of the track to let the next loaded car pass it … Close behind the first gang come the gaugers, spikers and bolters, and a lively time they make of it … Three [hammer] strokes to the spike. There are ten spikes to a rail, four hundred rails to a mile, eighteen hundred miles to [California]—twenty-one million times are those [hammers] to be swung—twenty-one million times are they to come down … before the great work of modern America is complete.*[1]

1. Quoted in Grenville M. Dodge, *How We Built the Union Pacific Railroad*. Big Byte Books, 2016. PDF e-book.

most important job was laying track. Workers first graded a smooth bed for the railroad, a job that required workers to level and move huge amounts of earth with pickaxes, shovels, horses, and mules. They then put down the track on which the railroad ran—thick wooden ties embedded firmly in the ground and iron rails that weighed 700 pounds (318 kg) apiece. The rails, moved by gangs of men, had to be lowered onto ties and secured with iron spikes driven into the earth with sledgehammers.

More than 10,000 workers built the Union Pacific Railroad. The workforce was mostly made up of former Civil War soldiers, Irish immigrants, and freed

This photograph, taken near Laramie, Wyoming, in 1868, shows a work crew laying a rail down on a bed of ties. This was a difficult task.

slaves. One of the hardest jobs was transporting tons of food, iron spikes, and other supplies workers needed for construction and to stay alive in the wilderness. As the workers made their way west, trains delivered most of what they needed to the end of track, where the rails stopped and new construction began. Forty train cars were required to carry enough material to build 1 mile (1.6 km) of track. Those supplies then had to be hauled several miles by wagon from the end of track to the site of new construction. To move those wagons, the Union Pacific used at least 10,000 horses, oxen, and mules.

Delivering supplies was a complicated job in itself. However, Dodge claimed

Union Pacific employees are shown here standing in front of one of the many supply trains used to keep construction running smoothly.

that the Union Pacific never ran into any major supply problems: "The work was so systematically planned and executed that I do not remember an instance in all the construction of the line of the work being delayed a single week for want of material."[43]

Most of his backbreaking labor was conducted in the wilderness. To ensure that workers would not quit because they missed the comforts of civilization, the Union Pacific did what it could to make their lives comfortable.

Life on the Rails

The workers were followed by a work train. The work train housed and fed the men. It had kitchens where simple meals—mostly meat, beans, bread, and coffee—were prepared. Much of the meat came from herds of cattle and pigs that trailed the construction crews through the Great Plains. The railroad also employed hunters to shoot bison that roamed the plains. Giant herds of these massive animals sometimes slowed work when they wandered

Hard Labor

Union Pacific Railroad workers had to do hours of challenging physical labor every day for just a few dollars. Author and historian Stephen Ambrose described the work of the men who built the railroad:

> *They had taken on a job that is accurately described as backbreaking … A day's routine was something like this: In the morning the men were up at first light. After [they got ready] they … had a hearty breakfast, and went to the job, whether plowing, shoveling, placing ties or rails, spiking them in, or putting on the fish-plates at the junction of two rails. At noon, "Time" was called and they had an hour for a heavy dinner that included pitchers of steaming coffee, pans of soup, platters heaped with fried meat, roast meat, potatoes, condensed milk diluted with water, and sometimes canned fruit … Then back to work, with the bosses cursing … to overcome the noontime [laziness]. "Time" was called again an hour before supper, to allow some rest. The evening meal was more leisurely. Then to the bunkhouses, for card games, a smoke, lots of talk [and] perhaps a song … Then to bed, the whole [process] to be repeated the next day and the next and the next.*[1]

1. Stephen A. Ambrose, *Nothing Like It in the World: The Men Who Built the Transcontinental Railroad 1863–1869*. New York, NY: Simon & Schuster, 2000. PDF e-book.

across construction sites in their search for food.

Workers slept in tents or railroad cars fitted with bunks. E. C. Lockwood, a teenager who worked on the railroad, claimed he found a better place to sleep than inside the cars, which were dirty and smelly. "To tell the truth," he said, "we were troubled by 'cooties' [bugs], and a companion and myself escaped them by making our bed between two skylights on the roof."[44] The two friends improvised a shelter out of a piece of tent cloth to protect them from rain and snow.

As the Union Pacific progressed westward, workers established base camps about every 70 miles (113 km) along the route. Some flourished into small communities because of an influx of gamblers, tavern keepers, merchants, and settlers. Most of these

By 1876, the camp of Cheyenne, Wyoming—pictured here—had already grown into a small town.

communities were temporary, but others grew into permanent towns, such as Cheyenne, the capital of Wyoming. Dodge and his survey crew laid out a site for Cheyenne in 1867, when the area was part of the Dakota Territory.

The railroad communities were called "Hell on Wheels" because there was so much crime and violence, most of it connected with drunkenness. In 1867, journalist Henry Morton Stanley described what life was like in one of these communities: "I [truly] believe that there are men here who would murder a fellow-creature for five dollars … Not a day passes but a dead body is found somewhere in the vicinity with pockets [robbed] of their contents."[45] This town, named Julesburg, got so out of control that Dodge sent Jack Casement and some workers back to do something about the drunks and gamblers who had violently taken over the community. When Dodge later went to Julesburg, he asked Casement what he had done. "I will show you,"

Casement said. He led Dodge to a cemetery and said, "General, they all died in their boots, but brought peace."[46]

Looking Back with Satisfaction

The workers who sometimes let off steam in the Hell on Wheels towns also worked very hard to build the transcontinental railroad. Dodge knew they had many faults, but he also admired their dedication and work ethic. Though the Union Pacific got off to a slow start, the rail line was being laid at unprecedented speeds. When the railroad was finished, Dodge said he thought the Union Pacific had built the best railroad possible:

> *When you look back to the beginning [with] everything to be created, with labor scarce and high, you can all look back upon the work with satisfaction and ask, under such circumstances could we have done more or better?*[47]

Chapter Five

THE CENTRAL PACIFIC HEADS EAST

To the West, the Central Pacific faced plenty of its own difficulties. While the Union Pacific had few geographical troubles, the Central Pacific had to battle nature. California had much to offer settlers, including a temperate climate; abundant natural resources, such as gold and silver; and plenty of fertile farmland. However, the area was cut off from the rest of the country by the massive Sierra Nevada range.

Though Theodore Judah had identified the Donner Pass as the ideal crossing for a railroad through the Sierra Nevada, many did not believe the formidable mountains were passable. After all, the Donner party did not have an easy time of crossing, and they did not have to lay miles of rail. Fortunately, the Big Four believed in his dream and his careful planning.

Judah's years of work to get a transcontinental railroad started came to a major turning point on July 1, 1862, with the signing of the Pacific Railroad Act. He famously sent a message to the Big Four: "We have drawn the elephant. Now let us see if we can harness him up."[48] The Central Pacific was the elephant. Judah wondered if this gigantic beast could actually be brought to life. Judah himself took charge of obtaining the initial supplies, including eight locomotives. This railroad engineer would devote the rest of his short life to his beloved transcontinental line.

The Problems of the Central Pacific

The Central Pacific broke historic ground on January 8, 1863, in Sacramento. The *Sacramento Union* newspaper claimed the ceremony was "of vast significance" because it marked the beginning of "the California link of the continental chain that is to unite American communities now divided by thousands of miles of

Railroad laborers are shown here making the route level so tracks could be laid for the Central Pacific.

trackless wilderness."[49]

The progress of construction was slow at first for the same reasons the Union Pacific struggled—namely, a manpower shortage and lack of financing. Acquiring iron rails, locomotives to pull trains, and other equipment was a severe challenge for the Central Pacific. In addition to shortages of such materials because of the Civil War, all of it was manufactured in eastern states and had to be sent to California by ship. That was not only expensive, but also took several months, which delayed the start of construction. The first rails did not reach California until October 1863, ten months after the groundbreaking, and the first rail was not laid until October 26.

By February 29, 1864, the Central Pacific had managed to build 18 miles (29 km) of track from Sacramento to Roseville, California, which allowed train service to begin between the cities. Then construction stopped because the railroad ran out of money. The Big Four investors had exhausted their credit and were unable to raise more money because many believed the transcontinental railroad was a risky investment.

Later that year, Lincoln made two decisions that eased the financing problem. He approved amendments to the Railway Act that increased the land the Union and Central Pacific were given for building the railroad and made it easier for them to sell bonds to raise money. Lincoln also took an action that specifically aided the Central Pacific. The Railway Act gave railroads $16,000 in loans for each mile of track in flat areas and $48,000 in mountain regions. Judah, the railroad's chief engineer, had determined the Sierra Nevada began at Barmore Creek, which was 31 miles (50 km) from Sacramento. Other Central Pacific officials wanted the mountain region to officially begin at Arcade Creek, which was only 7 miles (11 km) outside Sacramento, so they could receive the higher payments. This accounted for a difference of $768,000 in federal grant money.

The Central Pacific officials persuaded Josiah Whitney, a surveyor sympathetic to their financial struggles, to back up their claim about where the mountains began. Lincoln desperately wanted the project to succeed because he believed it would more solidly unite the nation, which was damaged by the Civil War. He went along with the new surveys, even though the area was not mountainous, and agreed that the higher payments would start

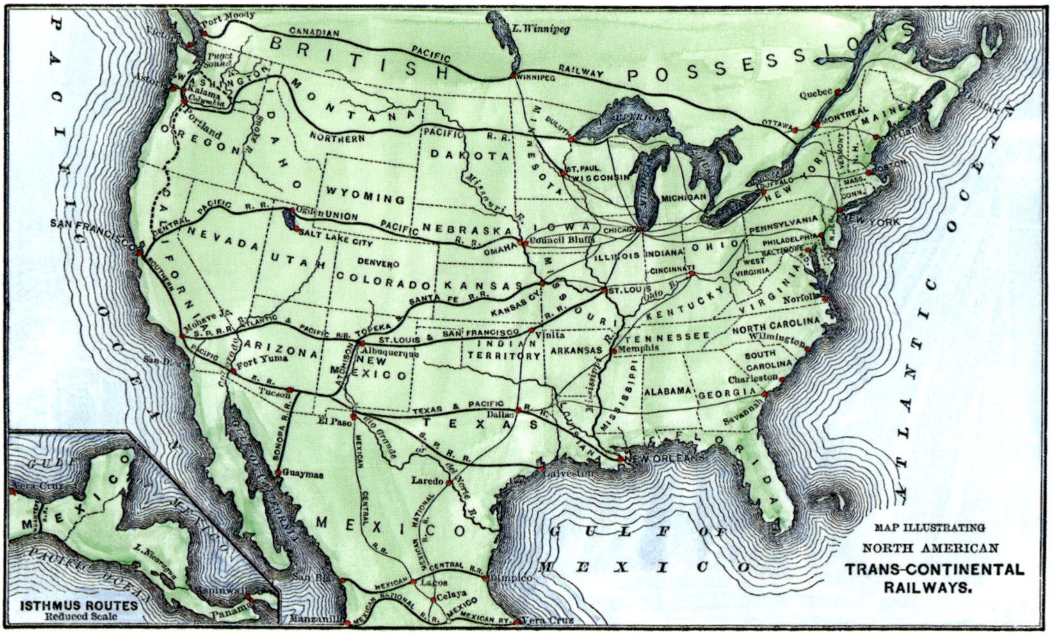

The complicated series of rail lines that ran across the United States by the end of the 19th century would never have become a reality without President Lincoln's decisions.

at Arcade Creek. When Lincoln signed his decision, he joked, "Here is a case in which Abraham's Faith has moved mountains."[50] In appreciation for Whitney's help in persuading Lincoln, the California legislature named the state's highest mountain after him—Mount Whitney.

The Central Pacific now had greater access to land and money, but it still lacked enough workers. The solution to this final problem provided a unique chapter in the nation's history.

Expanding the Workforce

In 1864, the Central Pacific had only 600 workers, far short of the thousands it needed to build a railroad. The lack of manpower slowed construction, and in its first 2 years, the railroad only laid 50 miles (80 km) of track. Like the Union Pacific, the Central Pacific faced a labor shortage because so many men were fighting in the Civil War. Many were also working jobs that were easier or paid more, including mining for gold and silver.

One source of labor the Central Pacific had not tried was Chinese immigrants, thousands of whom had come to the United States during California's 1848 gold rush. James Strobridge, a supervisor for the railroad, refused to hire Chinese workers because he prejudicially believed they lacked the strength, stamina, and skill to do the work. Many Americans at this time viewed the Chinese as inferior because of their skin color, smaller stature, and different customs and traditions, including non-Christian religions. Many white railroad employees created mocking and racist nicknames for their Chinese coworkers. Whites also restricted where the Chinese could live, shop, and eat; denied them citizenship; and sometimes beat or killed them without fear of being punished.

Charles Crocker, who oversaw construction of the Central Pacific, became so desperate for workers that he convinced Strobridge to try Chinese labor. Persuaded by his boss's demands, Strobridge hired 50 Chinese laborers in January 1865. After seeing them work hard for an extra-long first day on the job, Crocker sent a message to his office in Sacramento asking for more Chinese workers. In a few short months, the Central Pacific hired thousands of Chinese men. Soon, an overwhelming majority of its workers were Chinese. In September 1868, the *San Francisco Chronicle* reported, "At the present time, there are about 10,000 Chinese, 1,000 white men and [some] Indians employed on the [Central Pacific] road."[51] Although the railroad finally had enough laborers, it no longer had the man most responsible for making the transcontinental railroad a reality. After returning from Washington, D.C., in 1862, Judah and the Big Four began arguing about how to build the railroad, including its final route. Judah wanted the best and safest route, which was sometimes more expensive, while the investors favored the cheapest and quickest route. Judah also believed the Central Pacific had been morally wrong to make the

After putting aside racial discrimination, the Central Pacific found that its Chinese workers were an invaluable asset.

federal government agree that 25 miles (40 km) of flat terrain near Arcade Creek was mountainous just to make more money.

In addition to being the railroad's chief engineer, Judah was also a small investor in the railroad. In the summer of 1863, the Big Four grew tired of Judah's complaints. They forced him to sell his interest in the railroad and fired him. Judah was so angry that he decided to go to New York to seek investors to buy out the Big Four so he could build the railroad his way. During the long voyage back east, however, Judah fell ill. He died in New York on November 2, 1863.

The man most responsible for the transcontinental railroad never lived to see it completed. However, because of the labor of Chinese employees of the Central Pacific, Judah's dream would become a reality.

An Explosive Approach

It was fairly easy for workers to lay track for the first 30 miles (48 km) from Sacramento because the terrain, despite Josiah Whitney's report, was fairly level. Work became increasingly difficult over the next 100 miles (161 km) as the land gradually rose 7,000 feet (2,134 m) to the peaks of the mountain range. The Union Pacific had a fairly easy time crossing the Black Hills and Rocky Mountains, but the Central Pacific struggled at nearly every point of the route that snaked through the Sierra Nevada.

The Central Pacific had to tunnel directly through some peaks to lay track. In all, the railroad carved 15 tunnels with a total length of 6,213 feet (1,894 m), the longest being the 1,695-foot (506 m) Summit Tunnel. To do this, the workers used dangerous explosives to blast through solid rock. Chinese workers proved to be skilled at this task because they knew how to handle explosives and were unafraid to perform this dangerous work.

Workers drilled holes into solid rock, filled them with gunpowder, lit the fuses, and then ran to escape the blast. However, the mountain stone was so hard that workers could only lengthen a tunnel by 8 inches (20 cm) in 24 hours of blasting. The railroad eventually began using nitroglycerin, a chemical explosive several times more powerful than gunpowder, and the work went more quickly. Treasurer of the Central Pacific Mark Hopkins was delighted with one report of how well the new explosive was working: "Charles [Crocker] has just come from the tunnel and he thinks some of them are making three feet per day. Hurrah for nitroglycerine!"[52] However, the chemical explosive was extremely unstable. It sometimes injured and killed workers when it blew up accidentally, and railroad officials quit using it because of these safety issues.

Even more difficult than blasting tunnels through mountains was carving a path down the sides of Cape Horn, a wall of rock that rose 2,200 feet (671 m) above the American River. This project was initially considered impossible because no one knew how to get workers down the steep sides of the rock wall to blast the path. However, a Chinese worker told Strobridge how workers had built complex structures along the steep cliffs near the Yangtze River in China for hundreds of years. The technique was simple but dangerous: Workers in waist-high baskets woven from reeds were lowered down the side of the mountain using ropes. They drilled blasting holes and lit the fuses while hanging in the baskets. Then they were hauled up by hand

CENTRAL PACIFIC RAILROAD.

No. 1, TIME CARD No. 1.

To take effect Monday June 6th, 1864, at 5 A. M.

TRAINS EASTWARD.						TRAINS WESTWARD.		
Frt and Pass No 3	Frt and Pass No 2	Pass & Mail No 1.		STATIONS.		Frt and Pass No 1	Pass & Mail No 2.	Frt and Pass No 3.
5 P M leave	1 P M leave	6.15 A M, L	......	Sacramento.	......	8.45 A M arr	12 M arr.	6.40 P M ar.
5.50 5.55 } mt frt	2.15	3.55.	18	Junction.	18	3	11.20	5.55 5.50 } mt. Ft
6.09	2.38	7.05	22	Rocklin.	4	7.40	11.07	5.37
6.22	2.55	7.15 meet F	25	Pino.	3	7.15 mt pass	10.56	5.25
6.40	3.30 P M arr	7.30 A M arr	31	Newcastle.	6	3.45 A M, L	10.30 A M, L	5 P M, L

Trains No. 2 and 3 east, and 1 and 3 west, daily, except Sunday.

Trains No. 1 east and 2 west, daily.

LELAND STANFORD, President.

This is one of the first time cards for the Central Pacific line, which officially came into use in 1864 to transport passengers from Sacramento to Newcastle, California.

before the explosion. Many workers were injured from flying debris from the blasts, but they were brave enough to do the work.

A succession of thousands of blasts over months created a stone path from the cliff that was wide enough to support a train. A journalist awed by the constant explosions described their effect:

> *Huge masses of rocks and debris were … heaved up in the commotion … as if the whole artillery of Heaven was in play. Huge masses of rock rolled far down the steep [cliff face], and pieces weighing two hundred pounds were thrown a distance of a mile.*[53]

The Chinese labored for months to complete the difficult job, finally finishing the work by wielding pickaxes and shovels to smooth a path for the tracks. During those cold months, they faced other dangerous working conditions that made their job even harder: heavy snow and freezing cold.

Important Employees

The thousands of Chinese the Central Pacific employed proved themselves to be great workers. California governor Leland Stanford was one of the major investors in the Central Pacific Railroad. On October 10, 1865, Stanford wrote U.S. president Andrew Johnson about the progress of the railroad's construction. In the report, he praised the Chinese workers for their

Mormons and the Railroad

The culturally diverse enterprise of the construction of the transcontinental railroad also included Mormons. Utah's Mormon community was the first to benefit from the railroad construction, as it connected their settlements. Their leader, Brigham Young, signed a contract with both the Central and Union Pacific to lay lines across Utah (though only one would be used).

Because of their religion, Mormon workers did not drink alcohol or engage in gambling; they were dedicated workers. In an 1890 history of Utah, Hubert Howe Bancroft claimed: "It was acknowledged by all railroad men that nowhere on the line could the grading compare in completeness and finish with the work done by [the Mormon workers]."[1]

1. Quoted in Stephen Ambrose, *Nothing Like It in the World: The Men Who Built the Transcontinental Railroad 1863–1869*. New York, NY: Simon & Schuster, 2000. PDF e-book.

dedication to their jobs and claimed the transcontinental railroad could not be built without them.

The Chinese lived separately from the other workers and cooked their own food, which they bought and paid for out of their wages. Instead of the basic diet of beef and potatoes that the other workers ate, they dined on beef and pork, a variety of vegetables and fruit, dried seafood, and rice. They also drank hot tea all the time. Because the tea was boiled, the Chinese did not get sick as often as other workers who drank water, which was frequently contaminated with dirt or bacteria. On their day off, many Chinese workers smoked opium, a drug popular in China but not in the United States. Many also did something that was not customary at the time—bathing daily. Most white workers bathed once a week or even less.

Death in the Mountains

It took the Central Pacific more than two years to force a path through the Sierra Nevada. Workers frequently suffered from sickness and frostbite and many died during two of the worst winters anyone could remember. That first winter, from 1866 to 1867, there were 44 snowstorms, including a blizzard that lasted for 2 straight weeks and dropped more than 6 feet (1.8 m) of snow on workers before it ended.

Massive snowdrifts covered the worksites. Nearly half of the Central Pacific's workforce labored to keep the track shoveled so work could continue. It was expensive, but necessary, as Central Pacific official Arthur Brown explained:

> *It was decided … that the only positive means of protecting the road was by means of snow sheds and galleries, although the expense of building a shed nearly forty miles in length was [disgusting], and unprecedented … in railroad construction … It became a matter of the most vital importance that the sheds should be so far finished that the supplies and building materials for construction … should not be interrupted.*[54]

During its second winter in the mountains, the Central Pacific started to build 37 miles (60 km) of snow sheds—each structure was an extremely long roof—to keep the tracks clear of snow so work could continue.

Dozens of workers, many of them Chinese, died or got terribly sick from the cold. Many also died in avalanches when huge walls of snow slid down the Sierra Nevada's steep slopes, carrying away the shacks workers lived in and burying them alive. There were so many deaths during the winter months that it was not unusual to find a dead body on the side of the road while traveling. A.P. Partridge, an engineer who built bridges over ravines and valleys, was traveling in a sleigh with other workers when they came upon a dead man. Partridge wrote:

> *We saw something under a tree by the side of the road, its shape resembling that of a man. We stopped and found a frozen Chinese. As a consequence, we threw him in the sleigh with the rest of us, and took him into town and laid him out by the side of a shed and covered him with a rice mat.*[55]

The official records were not well kept, but it is believed that as many as 1,200 Chinese workers died during construction. These workers' sacrifices were not for nothing, however. It was their hard work that finally enabled the railroad to emerge from the mountains and descend to the Nevada desert in the spring of 1868.

Quickening the Pace

In January 1868, Crocker predicted that the Central Pacific would build "a mile a day for every working day in 1868."[56] That seemed an impossible goal for a railroad that had only set down 131 miles (211 km) of track in 5 years, but he knew workers would face easier conditions once they left the Sierra Nevada later that year.

The Central Pacific wanted to speed up construction because it was in a race with the Union Pacific. Both railroads wanted to lay as many miles of track as they could so they could get as much money and land from the government as possible for building the transcontinental railroad. Stanford wrote to Hopkins urging crews to work faster: "Have Charley [Crocker] double his energy, and do what is necessary to secure what labor is required to

Trestles, such as this one, allowed the Central Pacific workers to lay tracks throughout the Sierra Nevada. These would later be replaced with more sturdy structures.

push the road to its utmost. Anything less than the most that can be done will very likely end in defeat."[57]

One reason the Central Pacific was able to lay track so quickly is that it was not slowed by frequent Native American attacks. It created friendships by hiring Native Americans as workers, including some women, who shoveled dirt and swung sledgehammers alongside the Chinese. It also signed treaties with several groups that gave them free train rides. Working together reduced violence.

The railroad was constructed quickly across Nevada and into Utah as crews worked from dawn to dusk six days a week. To meet the needs of so many workers, thousands of people followed in railroad cars and wagons full of supplies. Cattle also followed, providing beef for meals. At the end of each day, at the end of finished track, a small community popped up, and this enabled the Central Pacific to feed and house its workers and

Trouble, Then Truce

In the final weeks of construction, the Central and Union Pacific were building track alongside each other. The Union Pacific crews had many Irish workers, while Chinese workers dominated the Central Pacific. Dodge, who witnessed the work firsthand, explained how this resulted in violence:

> *[In April 1869] each company graded a line, running side by side, and in some places one line was right above the other. The laborers upon the Central Pacific were [Chinese], while ours were Irishmen, and there was much ill feeling between them. Our [Irishmen] were in the habit of firing their blasts in the cuts without giving warning to the [Chinese] on the Central Pacific working right above them. From this cause several [Chinese] were severely hurt. Complaint was made to me by the Central Pacific people, and I endeavored to have the contractors bring all hostilities to a close, but for some reason or other, they failed to do so. One day the [Chinese], appreciating the situation, put in what is called a "grave" on their work, and when the Irishmen right under them were all at work let go their blast and buried several of our men. This brought about a truce at once. From that time the Irish laborers showed due respect for the [Chinese], and there was no further trouble.*[1]

1. Quoted in Union Pacific Corporation, "Historical Overview: Construction," Union Pacific Corporation, www.uprr.com/aboutup/history/hist-ov/hist-ov4.shtml.

equip them for the following day's work. In an 1868 article, the *Alta California* newspaper described how quickly these makeshift communities would disappear the next day:

> *The big settlement literally took up its bed and walked. The place that knew it at morning knew it no more at night. It was nearly ten miles off and where was a busy town of 5,000 inhabitants in the morning, was a deserted village site at night, while a smooth, well built, compact road bed for traveling stretched from the morning site to the evening [resting] place.*[58]

As the Central Pacific advanced steadily eastward, the Union Pacific hurried westward with equal determination. Between March and April 1869, crews from the two railroads finally met. Instead of stopping, however, they kept building parallel tracks past each other.

Smashing Records

The railroads continued construction after passing one another because the federal government had not yet decided on a meeting point where they would stop. Eager to lay more miles of track to get more money and land, the railroads began surveying and building overlapping railways. They worked so closely to one another that debris from explosions by one railroad crew to remove rocks would hit workers from the other railroad. Workers sometimes calculated the blasts to harass their rivals.

Realizing that the railroads were wasting money and delaying completion of the project, officials of the two railroads and members of Congress met to select a point to connect the transcontinental railroad. In April 1869, an agreement was reached to bind the tracks together at Promontory Summit, which is 56 miles (90 km) west of Ogden, Utah. The two railroads then had to change their routes and start heading there.

The railroads adjusted their courses as swiftly as possible because they would soon profit from ticket sales in stations they built in various communities. For example, the Union Pacific beat its rival to Ogden, Utah. The Union Pacific boasted about that, as well as having laid 4 miles (6.4 km) of track in 1 day in 1868. This angered Crocker, who told Strobridge to smash that one-day track laying record. The Central Pacific did it by laying 6 miles (9.7 km) of track, only to have the Union Pacific counter with a 1-day burst of 8.5 miles (13.7 km). Crocker wanted to break the record again by laying 10 miles (16 km). Strobridge told him, "Mr. Crocker, we cannot get men enough onto the track to lay ten miles." Crocker replied, "I've been thinking over this for two weeks, and I have got it all planned out."[59]

Crocker did not want the Union Pacific to get another chance at the record, so he planned to break it only a few weeks before the transcontinental railroad was to be joined in Promontory Summit. He used 4,000 men and several trains in an elaborate plan that rushed workers and supplies to the track site more quickly than ever. After one train unloaded, it backed up and allowed another train to go forward with more iron rails and other items. Workers formed long lines to carry and haul the equipment to where it was needed, while others shoveled, leveled, and pounded out a track. The work started at 7 in the morning on April 28, 1869, and when the day ended, the Central Pacific had laid a record of 10 miles (16 km) of track.

The big push helped the Central Pacific achieve its ultimate goal, which was to reach Promontory Summit before the Union Pacific. It did that on April 30, prompting this mocking comment in the *Alta California* newspaper: "The last blow has been struck on the Central Pacific Railroad, and the last tie and rail were placed in position today. We are now waiting for the Union Pacific."[60]

Epilogue

COMPLETELY TRANSCONTINENTAL

On May 10, 1869, a crowd of about 500 people gathered in the desert at Promontory Summit to witness the completion of the transcontinental railroad. They cheered when the final two iron rails were lowered into place, one by workers from the Central Pacific and the other by a crew from the Union Pacific. The rails were placed on a wooden tie carved from a California laurel tree. Four ceremonial spikes were used to secure the rails to the tie—two made of gold from California, one of silver from Nevada, and a fourth made from an alloy of gold, silver, and iron from Arizona. In addition to the cheering onlookers, people in cities throughout the nation were excitedly awaiting a telegraph message that the railroad was finished. As the big moment approached, the telegraph operator at Promontory Summit warned other operators across the country to keep the line open by not sending any messages:

> *TO EVERYBODY, KEEP QUIET. WHEN THE LAST SPIKE IS DRIVEN AT PROMONTORY POINT, WE WILL SAY "DONE!" DON'T BREAK THE CIRCUIT, BUT WATCH FOR THE SIGNALS OF THE BLOWS OF THE HAMMER.*[61]

Thomas C. Durant of the Union Pacific and California governor Leland Stanford had the honor of driving home the final golden spike, set into a predrilled hole so they would only have to tap it into place. Just after noon, Stanford swung a silver-plated sledgehammer. He missed the spike and hit the rail, but the telegraph operator sent the signal anyway. As Durant and Stanford finished tamping the historic spike into place, the transcontinental railroad was truly completed.

The meeting of the railroads, laborers, and officials in 1869 marked a turning point in American history.

People across the country rejoiced that the railroad was finished. Church bells in many cities rang, a parade snaked through the streets of Chicago, and people celebrated in their own homes. Americans were excited because they believed the transcontinental railroad was important to their nation's future. The country was not even five years away from the Civil War, which had threatened to permanently divide the United States. The iron rails linking the East and West Coasts were symbolic of a new unity.

The transcontinental railroad fulfilled that wish and transformed the nation in many ways. Author and historian Stephen E. Ambrose believed Americans in the latter half of the 19th century experienced more drastic changes in how

The scene at the driving of the final spike of the transcontinental railroad was captured by artist Thomas Hill in this painting from 1881 titled The Last Spike.

they lived than any other generation in U.S. history. In addition to the abolition of slavery, Ambrose cited technological advances that altered their lives, such as electricity, the telegraph, and the telephone. He claimed the transcontinental railroad was the technological achievement that caused the most change. Ambrose wrote:

> *The locomotive was the first great triumph over time and space. After it came, and after it crossed the continent of North America, nothing could ever again be the same. It brought about the greatest change in the shortest period of time [in U.S. history].*[62]

More Settlers, New Communities

On July 4, 1867, the Union Pacific established Cheyenne, Wyoming, as a transfer point for men and supplies

Ruining Rails in the Race

The legacy of the transcontinental railroad rarely includes details about the tremendous waste that was created along the way. In the race to finish, the companies adopted many careless practices. The two sets of tracks laid side by side in Utah are just one example of the railroad corporations' competition to wring every last dollar from the government. They also sometimes used low-quality materials to save money. Because of this, many lines had to be torn up and rebuilt in the years that followed. In at least one incident, in 1869, poor workmanship resulted in death. A passenger recalled:

> *A bridge over Bitter Creek, just east of Green River, [was] built upon [a base] of soft sandstone [and] crumbled away under our train … the passenger-car, in which I was, was only saved by a stringer or beam of the bridge catching into the roof and holding … One passenger was killed and several more or less injured … The bridge as well as two others in the vicinity had been examined the day previous and pronounced unsafe.*[1]

1. Quoted in Dee Brown, *Hear That Lonesome Whistle Blow: The Epic Story of the Transcontinental Railroads.* New York, NY: Open Road Integrated Media, 1977. PDF e-book.

while building the transcontinental railroad. Within a few months, thousands of people moved there to start farms, ranches, and other businesses. Union Pacific chief engineer Grenville Dodge wrote to his wife about the rapid settlement of Cheyenne: "They are coming from all quarters and all expect to make a fortune; some no doubt will."[63] Along the route of the transcontinental railroad, dozens of towns and cities sprang up almost overnight.

The irony of such early development along the railroad is that opponents of the transcontinental railroad had claimed railroads were not necessary until an area was already settled. Illinois congressman Stephen A. Douglas had been among outspoken critics who stopped an earlier proposal for a cross-country railroad by arguing that railroads should follow settlement instead of coming before it.

Others realized that railroads were vital to establishing new communities. When the transcontinental railroad was finished, a Montana newspaper wrote: "The iron key has been found to unlock our golden treasures … With railroads come population, industry and capital, and with them come the elements of prosperity and greatness to Montana."[64] Settlers moved wherever railroads laid tracks because they needed this vital economic and transportation link to the rest of the nation. Trains brought them goods they could not produce; carried away grain, corn, and other crops they grew so they could make a living; and allowed them to travel freely.

Many western settlers bought land from the Central and Union Pacific. This was the land the railroads had received from the government as payment for building the transcontinental railroad. People wanted the railroad land because it was closest to the tracks that were crucial to their livelihood. The railroads also lured western settlers who did not have to buy land. The Homestead Act, passed in 1862, promised people 160 acres (65 ha) of free land if they moved to unpopulated areas out West. The railroad made it easier for them to move west—a train trip took a few days instead of several months—and provided them the transportation link they needed to succeed in their new lives. It is estimated that the presence of railroads in the late 19th century contributed to the settlement of 285 million acres (115 million ha) of land before the Homestead Act was repealed in the mid-20th century.

Despite the huge surge in westward settlement, not all people who rode the transcontinental railroad were settlers heading west. Many people took the train just to experience what it was like to travel across the country.

Passengers, Mail, and More

One day after the transcontinental railroad was finished, the first trains moved along its lines from Omaha to Sacramento. By being connected to other railroads in Omaha, Americans could now travel across the continent in about a week. In the two decades that followed, millions of Americans made the trip from coast to coast.

There were three classes of passenger service on the transcontinental railroad. First-class passengers rode in cars with plush seats, ate meals prepared by chefs, and went to bed in sleeping compartments. They traveled to view the beautiful sights of part of the nation that most people had never seen before. Passengers were stunned and humbled by the incredible scenery of the trail westward.

Among the first tourists to the West were Europeans, such as Polish novelist Henryk Sienkiewicz. During his visit in 1876, he was amazed at the colorful people who also traveled on the train. He wrote:

> *They are not elegant, carefully dressed [gentlemen], but bearded and mustached individuals dressed in ragged garments carrying dirty bundles and with revolvers stuck in their belts. Their talk is loud … and filled with profanity. Clouds of tobacco smoke*

This drawing was part of an advertisement for the transcontinental railroad. It symbolized how fast the train was compared with other modes of transportation.

> *rise to the ceiling of the coaches. Doors slam as they are opened and closed by strong hands.*[65]

The people he saw were settlers moving west or local residents making shorter journeys for business or pleasure. They bought tickets for second and third class, which were cheap. However, the cars these passengers rode in were not as comfortable as the first-class cars. Second-class cars had upholstered seats, and people slept upright in them. Third-class passengers had narrow wooden benches that offered little comfort. Passengers in second and third class brought their own food or bought something to eat when the train stopped at stations. During these stops, travelers got on and off and the train took on water and coal, which provided power for the steam locomotive that pulled it. In addition to passengers, trains transported mail and just about anything else, from bathtubs to horses. The freight the trains carried was as important in reshaping the nation as its passengers. With a greater ability to transport goods, the American economy saw immediate and long-lasting benefits.

A Boon to Industry and Economy

When Asa Whitney helped ignite a national dream of a transcontinental railroad in the 1840s, he believed it would make the United States richer by providing a transportation link to Asia. In 1869, a periodical titled *American Railway Times* also claimed that the transcontinental railroad would enrich the nation in this fashion:

> *The lighter and valuable traffic of China and Japan with Europe will be quite likely to come over the Pacific Railway; the teas, spices, silks, and a thousand other articles of Asiatic commerce, will seek this line in preference to those now in use.*[66]

The *Railway Times* believed American businesses would profit by carrying Asian merchandise from the West Coast to the East Coast, then shipping them to Europe. Though this never quite happened, the railroad did help the national economy grow. Settlers bought products from eastern companies while creating their own and shipping them back east. Sidney Dillon, who helped finance the Union Pacific, commented on this two decades after the railroad was finished: "None of us dreamed that the future of the Pacific roads depended on the business that would grow out of the [settlers] of the deserts it traversed."[67]

Cattle are shown here being loaded onto a Central Pacific train to be shipped across the country.

The most impressive new business that was created due to the transcontinental railroad was the cattle industry. Between 1865 and 1890, railroads shipped millions of heads of cattle east to people hungry for beef. Once railroads reached western areas, cattle ranchers began driving large herds to towns such as Abilene and Dodge in Kansas, where they were sold and put on freight cars bound for large cities, such as Chicago.

Cattle ranches needed workers to tend their large herds and drive them to railroad stations. These workers were called cowboys. A description of a trail drive by Edward C. Abbott, a Montana cowboy nicknamed "Teddy Blue," explained why the cowboy era was one of the most colorful in U.S. history: "After you crossed the Red River and got out on the open plains, it was sure a pretty sight to see them [cattle] strung out for almost a mile, the sun shining on their horns."[68]

The transcontinental railroad was so successful and important to the nation's economic growth that four more were built. There was the Atchison, Topeka, and Santa Fe Railway, completed in 1881. It started at Atchison, Kansas, and after joining with the Southern Pacific Railroad at Deming, New Mexico, it ran to Los Angeles. The Great Northern Railroad was the first transcontinental railroad built without federal aid. Finished in 1893, it ran from St. Paul, Minnesota, to Seattle, Washington.

The new transcontinental railroads, and many smaller ones that developed in the last half of the 19th century, created a vast network of railways throughout the nation that made life easier for people. For one group of Americans, however, the railroads meant an unwelcome end to their way of life.

Minority Difficulties

Native Americans had nothing to rejoice about when the transcontinental railroad was completed. Chief Red Cloud led the Sioux people from 1866 to 1868 in their unsuccessful fight to stop whites from taking over Wyoming when the advancing railroad made white settlers flock to the area. After his warriors were defeated by the U.S. Army, the chief said, "The white children have surrounded me and have left me nothing but an island. When we first had this land, we were strong, now we are melting like snow on the hillside."[69] The "island" Red Cloud referred to was a reservation the federal government forced the Sioux to live on.

Many Sioux, Comanche, Cheyenne, and Apache groups continued to fight white settlers and soldiers for several years because they considered them invaders who were stealing their land. The Native Americans scored some victories, including the Battle of the Little Bighorn in Montana on June 25, 1876, when a force of about 2,000 Sioux and Cheyenne warriors killed more than 200 members of the

Seventh Cavalry led by Lieutenant Colonel George Armstrong Custer. However, Native Americans lost more battles than they won, and eventually every tribe surrendered and was forced to live on reservations.

One reason why the Native Americans were not successful in their resistance was that the bison had nearly disappeared. They depended on bison, also called American buffalo, for survival. They hunted these massive animals for food and used their hides to make clothes, moccasins, and shelter. By 1890, it is estimated that only 1,000 of the 12 million bison that once roamed the Great Plains were still alive. The rest had been killed by white hunters for meat or hides or slaughtered simply because they were considered a nuisance by railroad workers and settlers.

White hunters killed tens of thousands of bison to feed workers building railroads, including the first transcontinental railroad. The most famous hunter was William Cody, who earned the nickname "Buffalo Bill" by killing 4,280 bison from 1867 to 1868 for the Kansas Pacific Railroad. In the late 1860s and 1870s, white hunters killed millions of bison for their hides but left the meat to rot. When herds crossed railroad tracks, people in trains would sometimes shoot them just for fun through the windows of railroad cars.

The Native Americans could not understand the senseless slaughter of animals they valued as an essential part of their life. Black Elk, a Sioux chief, explained how upset they were about the destruction:

> *I can remember when the bison were so many that they could not be counted, but more and more [whites] came to kill them until there were only heaps of bones scattered where they used to be … they just killed and killed because they liked to do that. When we hunted bison, we killed only what we needed.*[70]

Another group that did not fare well after completion of the transcontinental railroad was the Chinese portion of the workforce that helped build the Central Pacific line. Many whites were angry at the Chinese because they worked for less money than whites. There were groups formed to protest cheap Chinese labor, which they feared would lower wages for everyone. By 1870, more than 100,000 Chinese people lived in California. Whites began to attack them in the Chinatown section of the city where they were forced to live. Sometimes, whites killed Chinese people or burned their homes and businesses.

The anti-Chinese feeling spread in the years after completion of the transcontinental railroad, even though the Chinese had been instrumental in building it. In fact, most of the workers killed during construction were Chinese. In 1882, Congress passed the Chinese Exclusion Act, which banned the immigration of Chinese into the United States for a decade. Congress later

This painting shows the massive herds of bison that roamed the Great Plains for thousands of years before white settlers killed millions of them.

extended the act several times. It lasted well into the 20th century.

Overall, however, the transcontinental railroad was a positive development for Americans. However, in the 1870s, some Americans came to believe that the companies that built it had been paid too much for the work they did.

Scandal and Investigation

On September 4, 1872, the *New York Sun* carried a front-page story claiming that Thomas C. Durant and other Union Pacific executives had used illegal financing schemes to obtain millions of dollars more from the federal government than it cost them to build their railroad. The story also claimed the railroad company bribed congressmen to get what it wanted by giving them shares of stock in Crédit Mobilier of America, a company the railroad set up to raise money for construction. Massachusetts senator George Hoar boldly claimed, "Every step of that mighty enterprise [the transcontinental railroad] had been taken in fraud."[71]

Congress investigated the allegations. It was considered the biggest political and financial scandal of the 19th century, implicating Vice President Schuyler Colfax and congressman and future president James Garfield, but no one went to prison. Some congressmen claimed they had not received bribes, but gifts. The scandal raised doubts about whether the transcontinental railroad was worth what the government paid for it. Many Americans also were upset because in addition to money, the Pacific Railway Act of 1862 had also granted the railroads 33 million acres (13 million ha) of land and free access to all the natural resources on that land.

The Central Pacific did not appear to be wholly innocent of fraud either. However, a congressional investigation into its contracts and finances was halted when their record books were burned. It still is not clear whether this act was accidental or deliberate. Nonetheless, the Big Four were never charged with wrongdoing. Though none of the major players in the construction of the transcontinental railroad were given jail time, the Crédit Mobilier scandal stands as one of the most controversial corruption investigations in American history.

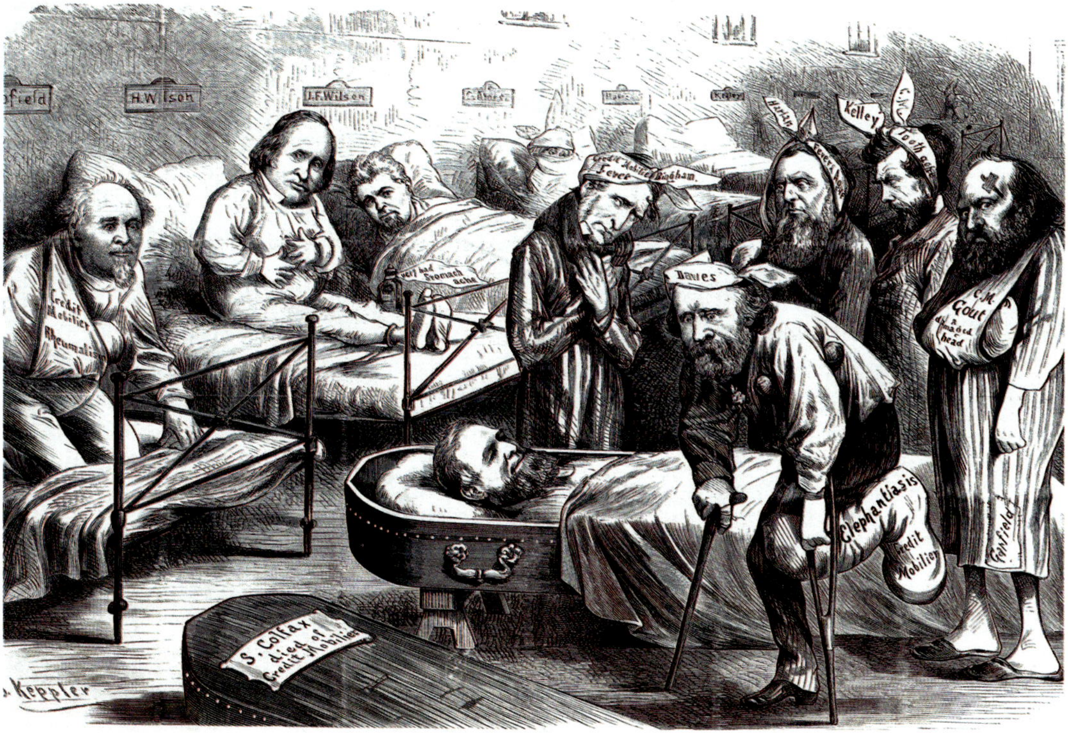

This political cartoon shows many of the influential figures involved with the scandal that surrounded the transcontinental railroad after its completion.

Weighing the Cost

Despite the scandals, historians today acknowledge that the transcontinental railroad was worth whatever the actual cost, even with profits illegally lining the pockets of investors and others. Eventually, both the Union and Central Pacific paid back their debt to the federal government, and the government benefited greatly by being able to ship freight and soldiers at a reduced rate. Some economists suggest the railroad helped elevate the stature of the United States around the world.

The transcontinental railroad has become a symbol of American innovation, determination, courage, and ambition. Yet this chapter in history also reveals dark details of greed, racism, and the destruction of natural resources. Even such notable figures as Theodore Judah were overshadowed by the scandalous and power-hungry corporations. On the day of the ceremony at Promontory Summit, at the celebration of the optimistic future that the railroad represented, Judah and his role were not acknowledged. His wife, Anna, reflected, "It seemed as though the spirit of my brave husband descended upon me and together we were there unseen, unheard of by man."[72] Historians, however, would not forget Judah's ingenuity, fortitude, and vision.

Though Judah vehemently disagreed with the corruption of the railroad corporations, his dream had been realized: The coasts were connected. The entirety of the U.S. railroad system—more than 140,000 miles (225,300 km) in operation today—continues to be crucial to the fabric of the American economy. The transcontinental railroad's contribution to the nation's dramatic transformation is undeniable.

Notes

Introduction: A Railway from Coast to Coast

1. Quoted in David Haward Bain, *Empire Express: Building the First Transcontinental Railroad*. New York, NY: Penguin Putnam, 1999, p. 124.
2. Quoted in Dee Brown, *Hear That Lonesome Whistle Blow: The Epic Story of the Transcontinental Railroads*. New York, NY: Simon & Schuster, 1994, p. 54.
3. Quoted in John L. Phillips, "Credit Mobilier." *American Heritage*, April 1969. www.americanheritage.com/content/credit-mobilier.

Chapter One: A Sprawling Nation

4. Luzena Wilson, "Luzena Wilson's View of the Overland Trek," Library of Congress. www.loc.gov/teachers/classroommaterials/presentationsandactivities/presentations/timeline/expref/oregtral/wilstwo.html.
5. Thomas Jefferson to James Monroe, 24 November 1801, Founders Online, National Archives. founders.archives.gov/documents/Jefferson/01-35-02-0550.
6. Quoted in Mary Sheldon Barnes and Earl Barnes, *Studies in American History*. Boston, MA: D.C. Heath & Co., 1893, p. 256.
7. Quoted in John F. Stover, *History of the Baltimore and Ohio Railroad*. West Lafayette, IN: Purdue University Press, 1987, p. 1.
8. William Cody in *The "Real" Wild West: First Hand Histories of the Old West*, Phillip J. Morledge, ed. Sheffield, UK: PJM Publishing, 2008, p. 282.
9. Quoted in William H. Goetzmann, *Exploration and Empire: The Explorer and the Scientist in the Winning of the American West*. New York, NY: Knopf, 1967, p. 271.
10. Quoted in Charles Henry Carey, *History of Oregon*. Chicago, IL: The Pioneer Historical Publishing Company, 1922, p. 679.
11. Quoted in PBS, "Asa Whitney (1791–1874) and Early Plans for a Transcontinental Railroad." PBS. www.pbs.org/wgbh/americanexperience/features/general-article/tcrr-whitney.
12. Quoted in Henry Nash Smith, *Virgin Land: The American West as Symbol and Myth*. Cambridge, MA: Harvard University Press, p. 28.
13. Quoted in Charles Frederick Carter, *When Railroads Were New*. New York, NY: Henry Hold and Company, 1909, p. 230.
14. Quoted in *Encyclopaedia Britannica*, "Manifest Destiny." www.britannica.com/event/Manifest-Destiny.

Chapter Two: Plotting a Course Across the Continent

15. Quoted in National Park Service, "Stephen Long," NPS, www.nps.gov/fosm/learn/historyculture/long.htm.
16. Quoted in Henry Martyn Field, *Our Western Archipelago*. New York, NY: Charles Scribner's Sons, 1902, p. 173.
17. Quoted in Gary Topping, *Utah Historians and the Reconstruction of Western History*. Norman, OK: University of Oklahoma Press, 2003, p. 161.
18. Quoted in Tom Chaffin, *Pathfinder: John Charles Frémont and the Course of American Empire*. Norman, OK: University of Oklahoma Press, 2014. PDF e-book.
19. R. S. Williamson, "The Williamson Report," in Gary Clayton Anderson, Laura Lee Anderson, ed., *The Army Surveys of Gold Rush California: Reports of Topographical Engineers 1849–1851*. Norman, OK: University of Oklahoma Press, 2015. PDF e-book.
20. Quoted in Robert Kent Fielding, *The Unsolicited Chronicler: An Account of the Gunnison Massacre, Its Causes and Consequences*. Brookline, MA: Paradigm Publications, 1993, p. 138.
21. Jefferson Davis, "Report of the Secretary of War," in *Reports of Explorations and Surveys to Ascertain the Most Practicable and Economical Route for a Railroad from the Mississippi River to the Pacific Ocean*, vol. 1. Washington, DC: Government Printing Press, 1855, p. 8.
22. Quoted in Susan Prendergast Schoelwer, "The Absent Other: Women in the Land and Art of Mountain Men," in *Discovered Lands, Invented Pasts: Transforming Visions of the American West*. New Haven, CT: Yale University Press, 1992, p. 128.
23. *Encyclopedia of North American Railroads*, s.v. "Judah, Theodore Dehone."
24. Theodore Dehone Judah, "A Practical Plan for Building the Pacific Railroad," Virtual Museum of the City of San Francisco. www.sfmuseum.net/hist4/practical.html.

Chapter Three: A Way to Preserve the Union

25. Theodore Dehone Judah, "A Practical Plan for Building the Pacific Railroad."
26. Quoted in Walter R. Borneman, *Iron Horses: America's Race to Bring the Railroads West*. New York, NY: Little, Brown and Company, 2010. PDF e-book.
27. Quoted in Georgie D. Runyan, *400 Years of America: Her Discovery, History, Achievements and Politics*. New York, NY: Cosimo Classics, 2010, p. 483.
28. Quoted in Stephen E. Ambrose, *Nothing Like It in the World: The Men Who Built the Transcontinental Railroad 1863–1869*. New York, NY: Simon & Schuster, 2000. PDF e-book.
29. Quoted in Bain, *Empire Express*,

pp. 109–10.
30. Quoted in Stephen E. Ambrose, *Nothing Like It in the World*.
31. Quoted in David Dary, *The Oregon Trail: An American Saga*. New York, NY: Oxford University Press, 2004, p. 282.
32. Quoted in R. Conrad Stein, *The Incredible Transcontinental Railroad*. Berkeley Heights, NJ: Enslow Publishers, Inc., 2012, p. 28.
33. Quoted in W. F. Bailey, "The Story of the Union Pacific." *Pacific Monthly*, July–December 1908, p. 67.
34. Quoted in Bill George, *Rails, Tales and Trails: A Step-by-Step Guide to Secret Locations, Fascinating People and Historic Towns of the Old Central Pacific Railroad from Sacramento to Reno*. November 7, 2013, p. 35.
35. Quoted in Bain, *Empire Express*.

Chapter Four: The Union Pacific Heads West

36. Quoted in Brown, *Hear That Lonesome Whistle Blow*, p. 61.
37. Quoted in PBS, "Oakes Ames (1804–1873)," PBS. www.pbs.org/wgbh/americanexperience/features/biography/tcrr-ames.
38. John Pope to R. M. Sawyer, 1 August 1865, *The War of the Rebellion: A Compilation of the Official Records of the Union and Confederate Armies*. eHistory. ehistory.osu.edu/books/official-records/102/1151.
39. Quoted in George Bird Grinnell, *The Fighting Cheyennes*. New York, NY: Charles Scribner's Sons, 1915, p. 257.
40. Quoted in Henry Latham, *Black and White: A Journal of a Three Months' Tour in the United States*. London, UK: Macmillan and Co., 1867, p. 286.
41. Quoted in Geoffrey C. Ward, *The West: An Illustrated History*. Boston, MA: Back Bay Books, 1996. PDF e-book.
42. Quoted in Ambrose, *Nothing Like It in the World*.
43. Grenville M. Dodge, *How We Built the Union Pacific Railway: And Other Railway Papers and Addresses*. Council Bluffs, IA: Monarch Printing Co., 1910, p. 16.
44. Quoted in Griswold, *A Work of Giants*, p. 168.
45. Henry Morton Stanley, *My Early Travels and Adventures in America and Asia*, vol. 1. New York, NY: Charles Scribner's Sons, 1895, p. 166.
46. Grenville M. Dodge, *How We Built the Union Pacific Railway*, p. 119.
47. Grenville M. Dodge, *How We Built the Union Pacific Railway*, p. 49.

Chapter Five: The Central Pacific Heads East

48. Quoted in Dennis Drabelle, *The Great American Railroad War: How Ambrose Bierce and Frank Norris Took on the Central Pacific Railroad*. New York, NY: St. Martin's Press, 2012, p. 22.

49. Quoted in Cheryl Anne Strapp, *Sacramento Chronicles: A Golden Past*. Charleston, SC: The History Press, 2013.
50. Quoted in Stephen E. Ambrose, *Nothing Like It in the World*.
51. Quoted in George Kraus, "Chinese Laborers and the Construction of the Central Pacific," Central Pacific Railroad Photographic History Museum. cprr.org/Museum/Chinese_Laborers.html.
52. Quoted in H. W. Brands, *American Colossus: The Triumph of Capitalism, 1865–1900*. New York, NY: Anchor Books, 2010, p. 66.
53. Quoted in John Hoyt Williams, *A Great and Shining Road: The Epic Story of the Transcontinental Railroad*. Lincoln, NE: University of Nebraska Press, 1988, p. 162.
54. Quoted in Roscoe Conkling and William D. Shipman, *The Central Pacific Railroad Company in Equitable Account with the United States, Growing Out of the Issue of Subsidy Bonds in Aid of Construction*. New York, NY: Henry Bessey, 1887, p. 33.
55. Quoted in David Haward Bain, *Empire Express*, p. 247.
56. Quoted in Kraus, "Chinese Laborers and the Construction of the Central Pacific."
57. Quoted in Ambrose, *Nothing Like It in the World*.
58. Quoted in Ambrose, *Nothing Like It in the World*.
59. Quoted in Ambrose, *Nothing Like It in the World*.
60. Quoted in Ambrose, *Nothing Like It in the World*.

Epilogue: Completely Transcontinental

61. Quoted in PBS, "One People," New Perspectives on the West. www.pbs.org/weta/thewest/program/episodes/five/onepeople.htm.
62. Quoted in Ambrose, "The Big Road," *American Heritage*. www.americanheritage.com/content/big-road?page=show.
63. Quoted in Gilbert A. Stelter, "The Birth of a Frontier Boom Town: Cheyenne in 1867," *Annals of Wyoming* 39, no. 1 (1967), p. 10.
64. Quoted in Krys Holmes, *Montana: Stories of the Land*. Helena, MT: Montana Historical Society Press, 2008, p. 171.
65. Quoted in Timothy C. Losey, "The Trail of Private Losey: A Biographical Sketch of Anson E. Losey's Military Service 1881–84," Inman Family Genealogy. www.jinman.org/library/trail.html.
66. John A. Haven, ed., "The Atlantic and Pacific Railway," *Railway Times* 21 (1869), p. 158.
67. Quoted in James P. Ronda, "How Railroads Forever Changed the Frontier," *American Heritage*. www.americanheritage.com/content/america%E2%80%99s-frontier-forever-changed?page=show.
68. Quoted in Geoffrey C. Ward, *The West*.
69. Quoted in James C. Olson, *Red Cloud and the Sioux Problem*. Lincoln, NE: University of Nebraska Press, 1965, p. 105.

70. Black Elk, "Black Elk Speaks: Across the Big Water," First People. www.firstpeople.us/articles/Black-Elk-Speaks/Black-Elk-Speaks-Across-The-Big-Water.html.
71. Quoted in Matthew Josephson, *The Robber Barons*. San Diego, CA: Harvest Books, 1962, p. 165.
72. Quoted in PBS, "Biography: Theodore Judah (1826–1863)," PBS. www.pbs.org/wgbh/americanexperience/features/biography/tcrr-judah.

For More Information

Books

Kreck, Dick. *Hell on Wheels: Wicked Towns Along the Union Pacific Railroad*. Golden, CO: Fulcrum, 2013.
This book gives an in-depth look at the camp towns that followed along the Union Pacific line of the transcontinental railroad, discussing how these towns attracted some of the best—and worst—businesses and settlers.

Otfinoski, Steven. *Building the Transcontinental Railroad: An Interactive Engineering Adventure*. North Mankato, MN: Capstone Press, 2015.
This engaging history contains unique points of view from various people involved with building the railroad, and it makes discovering its important figures fun.

Solomon, Brian. *North American Locomotives: A Railroad-by-Railroad Photohistory*. Minneapolis, MN: Voyageur Press, 2012.
This is a visual history of trains and railroad companies, from the 1800s to today.

White, Richard. *Railroaded: The Transcontinentals and the Making of Modern America*. New York, NY: W. W. Norton & Co., 2011.
This work explains how early rail lines were the first truly powerful American corporations and how they set the standard for business today.

Willumson, Glenn G. *Iron Muse: Photographing the Transcontinental Railroad*. Berkeley, CA: University of California Press, 2013.
This detailed work examines the history of the transcontinental railroad by looking at the images and photographs that were taken before, during, and after its construction.

Websites

Central Pacific Railroad Photographic History Museum (www.cprr.org)
This site has historic photographs of the Central Pacific Railroad, plus entries about every part of the construction process.

Transcontinental Railroad (www.history.com/topics/inventions/transcontinental-railroad)
Maintained by the History Channel, this site offers a multimedia experience to help visitors learn more about the transcontinental railroad.

Transcontinental Railroad (www.pbs.org/wgbh/americanexperience/films/tcrr)
This PBS site has links to important and detailed information, such as the impact of the railroad on Native Americans and short biographies of important figures.

Union Pacific Railroad Museum (www.uprrmuseum.org)
This site has photographs and articles about the Union Pacific Railroad, including an informative timeline of major events.

"Where the Buffalo No Longer Roamed" (www.smithsonianmag.com/history/where-the-buffalo-no-longer-roamed-3067904/?no-ist)
This article, published in *Smithsonian* magazine, details how the transcontinental railroad had a major impact on wild bison populations.

Index

Picture Credits

Cover Ed Vebell/Contributor/Archive Photos/Getty Images; pp. 4–5 Otto Herschan/Stringer/Hulton Archive/Getty Images; pp. 6 (top), 47 (top right), 62 MPI/Stringer/Archive Photos/Getty Images; pp. 6 (bottom left, bottom right), 68, 70 North Wind Picture Archive; p. 7 (top left) Science & Society Picture Library/Contributor/SSPL/Getty Images; p. 7 (top right) BenFranske/Wikimedia Commons; p. 7 (bottom) traveler1116/E+/Getty Images; pp. 9, 19, 72, 84 Bettmann/Contributor/Bettmann/Getty Images; p. 11 Buyenlarge/Contributor/Archive Photos/Getty Images; pp. 12–13 Courtesy of the Architect of the Capitol; p. 16 DEA PICTURE LIBRARY/Contributor/De Agostini/Getty Images; pp. 22, 31, 43, 47 (top left, bottom left, bottom right), 54, 87 Courtesy of the Library of Congress; p. 25 CptKeyes/Wikimedia Commons; p. 30 Chumwa/Wikimedia Commons; p. 37 SreeBot/Wikimedia Commons; p. 38 Felix Lipov/Shutterstock.com; pp. 45, 51 Courtesy of National Archives Catalog; p. 57 Print Collector/Contributor/Hulton Archive/Getty Images; pp. 61, 67 Omikron/Science Source/Getty Images; p. 64 US National Archives bot/Wikimedia Commons; p. 75 Library of Congress/Contributor/Corbis Historical/Getty Images; p. 79 Charles Phelps Cushing/ClassicStock/Archive Photos/Getty Images; p. 80 GraphicaArtis/Contributor/Archive Photos/Getty Images; pp. 83, 88 Historical/Contributor/Corbis Historical/Getty Images.

About the Author

Therese Harasymiw has written more than 200 nonfiction books for young readers, including a previous book about the transcontinental railroad which incorporated math problems. Harasymiw has a Master of Education degree in English Education, was a high school literature teacher, and now works as an editor for Gareth Stevens, an educational publishing company. She, her husband Mark, and son Luke reside in Rochester, New York.